The Blackbox Internet Marketing Bible

By Myke Black

Edition 1
Version 1.8.8
Last updated 23rd August 2015

Cover illustration by Myke Black.

Table of Contents

Introduction

This book is the accumulation of years of experience in SEO and online marketing by Myke Black, Senior Web Engineer for Blackbox E-Marketing. Blackbox is a web design and online marketing company specialising in medical websites, online e-commerce and bespoke web application development.

Each chapter has been written to give enough depth to give a solid understanding of the particular topic, but due to the range of topics in this book, it is impossible to fully cover every aspect of internet marketing in one volume, so further reading is advised if you want to delve deeper into any subject.

The primary target audience for this book is assumed to have little or no prior knowledge of internet marketing. However, even experienced online marketing professionals will find something of use to them. Where possible, industry specific jargon has been explained sufficiently for the reader to be conversant in the subject of SEO and online marketing and will hopefully equip them for further research in the topics that interest them.

The book itself is broken down into 4 sections, each of which are self-contained guides on a different aspect of internet marketing. The first is a brief introduction to search engines, and is a good place to start even if you already know a lot about how search engines currently work.

And finally, thank you for buying this book. We hope you enjoy reading it and find it helpful. If you would like to send us feedback, please email us at info@blackboxecom.com.

Section 1 - What is Internet Marketing

This section is a general introduction to internet marketing and why you should be doing it. It begins with a look at how the internet went from being "the inter-what now?" to "I can't live without my WIFI – and I don't even know what it stands for!" and ends with a look at three dimensional marketing models. It's going to be a fast ride so hang on to your (hopefully white) hat!

Chapter 1 - Introduction to Internet Marketing

1.1 Hello World

Blackbox E-Marketing been in the business of web development and online marketing for the past 20 years in one form or another. Throughout this time, we've seen many changes in the online landscape. The pace of technological and online social change has been dizzying at times.

Remember the early days of the web, when the few of us who had access to this ephemeral plane were seen as a bit weird? Back then, Lego's website looked like this:

Fig. 1: Lego homepage from 1996 - source: archive.org

.. and digital watches were still thought of as a pretty neat idea.

At that time there were predictions of how the 'information superhighway' (as the late visionary Clive James called it) would revolutionise our lives. We had no idea then about how social media, online shopping, or online marketing would become so salient in our lives. When I think back to the early days of the World Wide Web, I'm always reminded of Richard Burton purring the opening words of Jeff Lynn's War of the Worlds. "No one would have believed, in the last years of the nineteenth century that human affairs were being watched from the timeless worlds of space..."

I think the sentence should end with "... by Larry Page and Sergey Brin"

1.2 Current State of Online and Offline Marketing

Fast forward to 2015, and we are in an increasingly connected world. The table below shows the number of UK households with internet access from 1998 – 2014:

Table 1 : Households with Internet access, 1998 to 2014

Year	%
1998	9
1999	13
2000	25
2001	36
2002	42
2003	46
2004	49
2005	55
2006	57
2007	61
2008	65
2009	70
2010	73
2011	77
2012	80
2013	83
2014	84

Source: Office for National Statistics
(http://www.ons.gov.uk/ons/rel/rdit2/internet-access---households-and-individuals/2014/rft-ia-2014.xls)

The rate of growth has been more or less linear and by 2020 it is estimated that 98% of the UK will be connected. Across the world, other poorer countries are slowly catching up, opening previously unavailable markets.

In contrast to the increasing use of the internet, there has been a steady decline in 'traditional' media: the number of people reading newspapers and magazines has falling since the 1970's, and the viewing figures for the terrestrial channels have dropped significantly in the last 3 or 4 years. The latter due in part to video on demand, YouTube, illegal downloads and the hundreds of satellite and cable channels you can now get cheaply (or free).

If you have a product or service you want to market to people, you can no longer rely on magazine ads or TV adverts alone. You need to target your efforts at where people are going to see them, not where they were looking before. In this sense, marketing is a bit like shooting clay pigeons. If you aim for where it was the last time you got a hit, you are likely to miss. If you aim for where the clay disk is now, you will certainly miss. To hit the target you have to predict where your target will be and pull the trigger at just the right time. Since people direct a significant amount of their attention towards online media, that's where you have to point your marketing gun. Online marketing used to be an afterthought to an ad campaign, now it is integral to marketing campaigns.

I've had a few jobs in the past where someone (usually a self-important marketing manager) would say "oh, we need a website for this advert that's going in the magazine, and we need it now, because the magazine is published today and the link to the website is in it" – a phrase generally met with rolling eyes, slapped foreheads and late nights for the poor web monkeys who typically inhabit the darkest corner of the trendy open-plan office.

Nowadays, you should always make the web presence perfect first. There's nothing worse than creating a lot of buzz about an event or product only to have the website fail to convert your visitors into paying customers because of a broken link or bad design. When your site is perfect you can then publish the ad using traceable links or QR codes (i.e. those funny square barcode things that no one uses but marketing managers just love 'em). Post to social media at the same time as the real world advertising launch to create a cross channel event. Online services such as Hootsuite (https://hootsuite.com) and Twitterfeed (http://twitterfeed.com/) can help make the process of simultaneous information dissemination a bit easier by posting content to all your social media at the same time as the content is posted to your website. These services are described in more details in the chapter "Social Media Marketing"

If your business is not marketing, you're not creating business. If your business is not marketing online, then your business will not create online business. It's not quite rocket surgery, but having a good awareness of internet marketing will help you create more business from a variety of online sources.

1.3 Three Dimensional Marketing

This book is mainly intended for the businessman (or woman) who might have heard of things like 'social media', 'SEO' or 'AdWords' but doesn't have a clue how to go about using these powerful tools to create more business. It will cover the 3 dimensions of online marketing:

1. **Search Engine Optimisation (aka on-site marketing)**

2. **Off-site Marketing**

3. **Conversion Marketing (the holy grail of IM)**

The coverage will go from the basic concepts to advanced strategies and tactics. Each dimension of online marketing is a distinct discipline with different skills and tactics required. If you are not interested in SEO (maybe you have a guy to do that for you) then you can skip the chapters on SEO but it is recommended that you read at least the first chapter to give you a good understanding of the basic principles. If you are an SEO practitioner and not too interested in customer lifecycle marketing, then there's no prize for reading stuff that you don't want or need to know – although if you paid for this book, it will make the cost per page a lot cheaper if you read all of it, that's all I'm saying.

Section 2 – Search Engine Optimisation

Section 2 is a big section covering all major aspects of search engine optimisation. If you are not interested in using SEO (then why are you reading this book?) you can skip to the next section, but I recommend that you read chapter 3 if you are unfamiliar with the concept of SEO.

Chapter 2 - The Evolution of Search Engines

2.1 What the Sam Hill is a search engine?

Search engines are websites or software that enables a person to find documents or other media on the internet. Most famous search engines are Google - originally called 'BackRub' and is now owned by parent company Alphabet - and Bing - originally known as MSN search. There are thousands of other search engines on the internet, but few are used by more than a handful of real world people. Here's the UK search engine market share from July 2014 to July 2015:

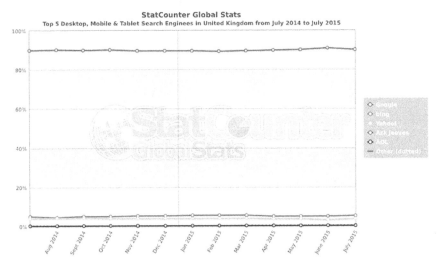

Fig 2: Top 5 search engines in UK July 2014 to July 2015 - source: statcounter.com

As you can see, Google pretty much has a steady 90% share. In the last few months that's gone down very slightly but not really worth the headlines that it has been getting ("Google loses market share following Mozilla's Yahoo switch", "January UK search market share: Bing continues increase" etc.). Make no mistake, Google is not completely safe, but if you are thinking of spending any time promoting your website to a UK audience. Google is the only search engine you need to consider. In the United States, the situation is pretty similar:

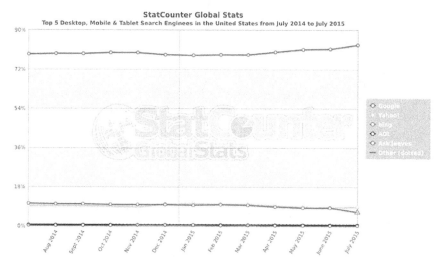

Fig 3 Top 5 search engines in the US July 2014 to July 2015 - source: statcounter.com

Google still holds the majority share at 78%, but about 22% of search engine usage is for the other 'major' search engines. And that trend does not seem to be changing an awful lot. There was a brief period recently when the Firefox browser changed its default search engine from Google to Yahoo, and Google market share wavered, but the evidence is that those users are gradually reverting back to Google (once they've finally figured out where the setting is in Firefox to do this). Similar effect was seen when Windows 10 was launched in July 2015 as people experimented with the new Edge browser. Edge uses Bing as the default search provider and to change this to google was not a simple task so people stopped using Edge shortly after upgrading to Windows 10.

So when we talk about search engines today, we can almost use the words 'Google' and 'search engine' interchangeably. In fact, the word 'search' in common language has been replaced with 'Google' – "I'll just Google the phone number for the restaurant" or "I just Googled myself, and immediately regretted it".

Once your brand replaces a verb or noun you know you've made it. Pre-internet examples of genericised trademarks include Hoover, Coke, Selotape and even Heroin (yes, really – trademarked by Friedrich Bayer & Co, 1898). These have now been joined in the digital age by Facebook, eBay and twitter (as in 'tweet'). I can't imagine anyone 'binging' a phone number or 'yahooing' recipes in the near future.

2.2 Generation 1 search engines – keywords rule!

In the old days of the internet, before Google ruled the world, (and I still had hair) search engines were very simple beasts. They were big databases of keywords with links and relevancy scores. The more 'relevant' a website was to a keyword, the higher the relevancy score, and so the higher up in search engines they would appear. The relevancy score was calculated purely on the content of the web page itself. To get high rankings in the search engine, all you had to do was decide which keyword you wanted to target, and make sure that keyword appears in your web page as much as possible - but not too much.

There were rules that you had to follow to get the perfect balance of keyword ratios: the title of your web page should contain between 7 and 12 words, and contain the keyword not more than 3 times. The keyword should appear in at least one heading, preferably twice, and you should have at least one image with the filename containing the keyword. The metatags should have your keyword in at least 6 times, and you should wear the keyword on at least 2 items of clothing at any time. OK I made the last bit up, but you get the gist.

If you had a web address containing the keyword that was even better. For example, having 'insurance.com' would have helped greatly if you were selling insurance products, and that is still partly true today. That's why the domain name insurance.com was sold for $35.6 million in July 2014. There's a lot of money that was made by preregistering domain names. Chris Clark, owner of a small software company, registered pizza.com in 1994 for the princely sum of $20. 14 years later he sold it at auction for $2.6 million. Not bad for just sitting on it for 14 years and paying the small annual renewal fees.

The sincerest form of flattery...

One of the easiest ways to get to the top of the generation 1 search engines was to look at the websites that were in the top 5 and just copy the number of keywords they had in their web pages. Easy peasy! You could get to the top of Alta Vista, Lycos or Ask Jeeves in a few weeks using this method. All you really needed to get included in the search engines was to submit your site to an 'add url' page on the search engine. This process was simplified by the development of search engine submission software that could submit your website(s) to thousands of search engines in a matter of minutes and you could schedule that submission to happen on a monthly basis – this helped in those engines which showed the latest submissions higher up in the list.

Life was easy for us SEO guys; you could almost guarantee top positions to your clients in a short space of time. Competition for keywords was relatively low then, as few people were using SEO to promote their sites. Not even the big companies bothered with it that much. Clients were happy, we were happy. Everything was hippy dippy until generation 2 hit...

2.3 Generation 2 search engines – backlinks rule

Google was launched in 1998 as a project in Stamford University using a new breed of 'spider'. This kind of spider was not the hairy scuttling thing that I'm frequently called on to remove from the bathroom, but the automated program that analyses links on webpages, then stores the addresses of the linked pages to analyse at a future date for inclusion into its index. Spiders appeared on the internet in the early 1990's but Google's spider was different from previous ones in that it used the information about links to web pages to influence the position of the web page in the search engine results pages (SERPs). The more 'backlinks' a site had, the more it was assumed that that site was an authority on the particular subject and so the better it's relevancy score. Other search engines quickly adopted this method.

This then changed the tactics of SEO generals. Their focus was no longer just on what was on their own web pages, but also on getting back links. Lots of backlinks. Link exchange schemes appeared and link directories started sprouting up. The more back links you could get to your site, the better your rankings were. Automated software was developed to create dynamic databases of links (We even made one or two such programs ourselves) and webmasters were emailing other site owners to ask for links to be added. SEO software even had tools to automatically generate polite sounding emails to other site owners to request a link on their site.

Foreign companies then got into the action. In particular, Indian SEO companies were being set up with just one product to create fake blog sites to give your site more backlinks. They would typically promise 100 backlinks per dollar with a minimum commitment of a few dollars per month.

Experiences with these companies were not generally very good. As soon as you stopped paying them, those backlinks would disappear or be redirected to other sites. These companies are still around today and we occasionally get spam messages from them which are instantly deleted.

Because of the increase in spam websites floating to the top of the search engines, Google added a new feature to the backlinks called Page Rank (PR) - named after Larry Page, one of the founders of Google. I guess 'Brin Rank' just didn't sound right.

Originally the concept was used in the Chinese search engine, Baidu and copied by Google. Page ranking allocates backlinks different amounts of 'weight' according to how popular each linking page is. This then meant that creating thousands of low weighted spam backlinks from 'ghost' pages and 'doorway' pages no longer had such an effect and the target page's ranking.

The way PR works under the hood is this: if a page has lots of links to it, it gets more 'link juice' (Google's word for it, not mine). The juicier a page is, the more powerful its links became (and also the better rankings in Google it has). However, at the same time, the more outbound links a page had, the more 'leaky' the page became, so the amount of link juice transferred to the pages it links to is reduced. To get a really juicy page, what you need is lots of juicy pages linking to yours which themselves don't have dozens of leaks out of them.

How link juice is transferred

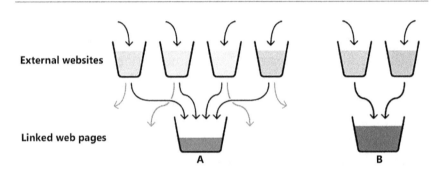

Fig 4: Link Juice Flow diagram - source:
http://blog.woorank.com/2013/05/the-flow-of-link-juice/

In the diagram above, we have 2 pages, A and B. A has twice as many inbound links than B so should normally have twice the amount of page rank. However, the external webpages that link to A are much more leaky than those that link to B so they pass on less juice. This effect passes on down the linking chain, so you will find that sites with good links from high PR pages have much higher PR themselves. That's why backlinks from high PR pages were much more valuable.

Since A is much more juicy than B, its links have much greater value. Note, there are ways to plug the link juice leaks in your page by using 'nofollow' links. These are covered in greater detail in "2.3 backlinks – the right and wrong way to do them".

Another aspect of link juice is that the links have 'flavours' – each flavour is associated with a keyword, so for example if you have lots of high PR pages linking to yours with the keyword 'socks' then your link juice for that keyword will be high, however your ranking for other words like 'hats' will not be increased as much by these links.

Google used to publish the page rank data for websites and made it available in their free browser toolbar. However, they realised that having this data made it easier for black hat SEOs and search engine spammers to manipulate the rankings, so they stopped updating the database and PR is now a secret part of the search engine's ranking systems.

2.4 Generation 3 Search Engines.

Remember the Socks and Hats thing in the last section? Well, generation 3 search engines are very clever. They can recognise whether two words or phrases are related concepts. So Google knows that Socks are a type of clothing and Hats are too, so links to a sock website from a hat website will have higher relevancy than links from a dentist's website.

How do the search engines do this? Well, they use a technique called 'latent semantic indexing' which uses mathematical techniques to discover patterns in related keywords by looking at their context. For example, if Google finds that on a lot of clothing websites the words 'socks' and 'hats' appear on the same page, then it can conclude that they are related terms. Google is just a robot, it does not comprehend the concepts of clothing or socks or hats; it just knows they go together. A bit like how my dog knows that the sound of running water from upstairs and the sound of me shouting down 'BATHTIME!' means at some point in the near future she's going experience something that she doesn't like much. Dogs have no idea what the word 'bath time' means, or that the sound of running water upstairs is the bath being filled. She just knows that it's probably a good time to hide under the dining table.

Generation 3 search engines, which is where we are currently, build up a keyword vocabulary (also known as a 'keyword theme') and uses this to determine relevancy. If you search for 'socks' then the top results in Google will be filled by pages that are **about** socks – whether the word socks appears on the page or not. Some pages just have 'underwear'. Some pages have 'footwear', but Google knows that they are related to socks and so they appear in the search results too.

To get good rankings in Google now you must concentrate more of your efforts into getting the content of your pages to contain this keyword vocabulary. If you stuff your page with 'socks, socks and more socks' the chances are Google will look at your site and think, "well, that looks a bit spammy" and reward you with lower rankings. One notable example of this was the EMD penalty that Google hit us with back in Sept 2012…

One cloudy autumn morning towards the end of 2012, I was just having a nice hot cup of tea while our SEO software was diligently running its end of month reports when I noticed that one of our client's sites had just plummeted in rankings from 2nd or 3rd in the results to nowhere overnight. I checked the rankings manually and confirmed that it wasn't a dodgy cup of tea that was making me see things, it really had disappeared from Google.

Previously this site was doing really well: we had good content, good keywords and quite a few backlinks with the keyword text in and had the specific keyword as the url too. This last part was the problem. The update in Google's search algorithm penalised sites with had the exact same domain name as the back links text.

This update was designed to hit those spammy websites selling Viagra and various other nefarious things. The spam sites often used keyword matching domain names like 'buyviagranow.com' and then built lots of backlinks with the same link text. So Google decided to turn its cannon against the practice.

In hitting the spam sites, the update also hit many sites that had been using white hat SEO to build traffic ('white hat' is what we call SEO that does not use underhand methods to get better rankings).

The moral of the story is, if you are thinking of registering a new domain name now, avoid using your keywords as the URL. Go for a brand name or something similar. Local domain names, like manchestershouldersurgery.com are also ok (so far), so if you have "welikebikes" that's fine. Having "newbikes.com" is probably not. This is the complete opposite of what worked well in generation 1 and 2 websites.

The advice now is to avoid using keywords in your link text, and try to have the backlinks appear on authority pages which are relevant to your site's content theme. A good idea is to have the title of the webpage that you are linking to as your link text. So if you had a page titled "choosing a suitable bike for your needs" and you wanted to put a link to it in another page, instead of:

"When buying a new bike, always consider the terrain you plan to ride on."

You should write the link as:

"When buying a new bike, always consider the terrain you plan to ride on – read more on 'choosing a suitable bike for your needs'."

Or you can just put the website address as the link, as in:

"When buying a new bike, always consider the terrain you plan to ride on – read more here: http://mykelikesbikes.com/advice/choosing-your-bike

Notice in the last link, the address of the page still has relevant keywords in – 'advice', 'choosing' and 'bike' are all themed to the topic of researching bikes. This method of creating urls is favoured by Google, and it also helps give people an idea of what your page is about just from the web address.

What I've found as a good rule of thumb when designing SEO strategies is that whatever helps your visitors and gives them a better experience on your site, also tends to help with SEO. Having logical site structures, making sure there are no broken links, making sure the site loads quickly, eradicating spelling mistakes and linking to and from good quality sources are all essential to getting good rankings (and thereby traffic) for your website.

2.5 Pandas, Penguins, Pigeons and other animals in the Google Zoo

You might have heard stories in the press about the "Google Panda update" or how "Google penguin hits online businesses" but what are these animals and why should they matter?

To answer this, we need to first explain how Google ranks websites. Each time you do a search on Google, your query is matched against a number of factors. Like a KFC recipe, the things that go into generating search results (the search algorithm) are a closely guarded secret. Supposedly there are over 200 different ingredients in the dish, each with different amounts of influence (although there are some people who counter this claim) Some possible influences on the rankings are: number of backlinks, power of backlinks, age of website, quality of content, content of meta tags, page loading speed, domain name extension (.ac and .gov domains are more trusted), social reputation, the list goes on.

The problem is no one can tell 100% which factors are in play at any time and what their relative importance is. If I knew the exact recipe, I wouldn't be writing this book. I would be relaxing on a beach in Mauritius with a mojito trying to imaging creative ways to spend all my money.

Even if you did find out what the most influential factors are, there is no guarantee that one of the inmates of Google's menagerie won't mess it up.

When Google releases an update to its search formula, often the first we know about it is when the rankings of websites change. Sometimes it's a minor change, sometimes there are big changes in ranking. Working in SEO is a bit like trying to sail a boat across the Atlantic. If you are lucky, then you will not have any problems, but if you get hit by a Google update, then it's like sailing in a typhoon. The best you can do is try to weather the storm and keep afloat in the top pages. The first few days after an update is when you notice the biggest peaks and troughs of rankings. This is sometimes called the 'Google dance' – where websites move up and down the rankings, switching places with other sites quite quickly. Generally after a few days, the storm eases, then you get to figure out whether you have done well or badly out of the update. As I write, there has been a minor update in the past few days and search engine experts are still discussing whether this is an undisclosed new update, or a tweaking of a previously released update.

Some of the major updates in the past couple of years have been given names. Here's a quick rundown on the updates, and what it has meant for SEO:

Panda – in terms of updates, this was a biggy. First released in Feb 2011, the effect of this update was to reduce the rankings of sites of low quality or thin content – sites with good quality content did well from this update. Sites  which relied mainly on backlinks to boost rankings did very badly. The first version reportedly changed the rankings of 12% of all websites – which is the largest ranking change ever recorded. There were numerous panda updates in the first couple of years but things slowed down after that, the last one recorded was September 2014.

Penguin – If you thought panda was bad, penguin was worse. Just like the nemesis of Batman, this update caused chaos in the SEO world. The first penguin update was April 2012. This update cracked down hard on websites that were seen to be manipulating  the rankings in violation of Google's webmaster guidelines (a code of good practice published by Google). One of the things targeted was link exchange schemes, or reciprocal linking. This is simply where one website links to another in exchange for a backlink in return. This practice was common in the early days of SEO, but is now a sure fire way to get penalised. Another practice now outlawed is the use of doorway pages – these are pages set up to focus on a narrow set of keywords created solely to generate keyword relevant backlinks to the main website.

According to Google's own figures, 3.1% of websites were affected by this update. That's still a big number considering the size of Google's index, but nowhere near the level of panda.

To date, there have been 6 versions of the penguin update, the final one was in October 2014 but more minor updates have been announced for the future.

Pigeon – This is the unofficial name for this update given by the SEO community and it reflects the fact that the update focuses on local search. The pigeon update was released in July 2014 and had the effect of improving the relevancy of local search results. This was good news for those sites that advertised local  business as it removed a lot of spam from local search. Changes also affected searches in Google maps and Google business.

Hummingbird – not really an update to the ranking algorithm per se, but an entirely new backend for the search engine, and replaced the earlier "caffeine" engine. Hummingbird was released in august 2013, and one of the focuses of the new system was to allow for semantic  search (searches that use context to generate meaning) and more natural speech processing. Previously, if you put into Google "where is the nearest pizza place to me" – the results would not always display the nearest pizza shops to you, but instead show those web pages which have the words 'nearest' and 'pizza' in the content. If you owned nearestpizza.com you could have got a lot of traffic. With hummingbird, natural text is translated into more accurate search queries by taking into account of the context of the text around it, so when you do the same search now, Google will attempt to use your location data to show nearby takeaways. Hummingbird was an essential update for the release of Google Voice. If you do a search for 'lead and collar' it will give you a completely different set of results to 'lead pipes'.

Avoiding being hit by Google Updates

The purpose of all Google's updates has been to remove the lower quality sites from the results that people get from search. Therefore if you don't want to be hit by another Google animal in the future, you have to create high quality sites with ethical and natural link building and good structure and avoid anything that might look spammy. It's as simple as that.

To learn how to make high quality content sites that Google loves, read the next chapter "Basic Search engine optimisation"

Like all bad handheld camera movies (with the notable exception of Trollhunter), I'll start this chapter with a quick disclaimer:

The advice you are about to read may not necessarily apply by the time you read this chapter. Search Engine Optimisation is not an immutable science and Google reserves the right to move the goalposts whenever they feel like it.

What was true only a couple of years ago might not apply now, so it is good practice to keep informed about the latest goings-on in SEO. There are many sites and news feeds you can subscribe to in order to do this. I recommend just googling 'SEO news' and check out the sites at the top of the list. After all, if they are top in Google for SEO news, then the chances are, they know what they are talking about.

3.1 First principles in SEO

Here are a few quick and simple principles which you should apply from the start of the SEO efforts:

1. **Focus Grasshopper**
   When starting SEO the first question you should ask is: 'what is your site about, and who is it for?' You need to have a clear idea about the purpose of your website. If your site is a random collection of different pages with maybe a forum, and maybe a gallery, and with maybe a couple of products linking to PayPal and maybe based around a range of different topics and interests, then your SEO will fail at the first hurdle. If you have a site designed to cater for different audiences, then you should really consider splitting your site into several more focused websites.

   To get a good, clear SEO strategy you need a site that is easy to classify. If YOU can't tell anyone in one sentence what your site is about, then Google, which is (one assumes) infinitely less clever than you are, will find it impossible to classify your site, and your pages will appear nowhere in the Google search engine results pages (SERPs).

2. **Make sure Google can read the content**
   Using flash for content or menus? That's sooooo bad!

Using images for navigation buttons? Tsk tsk. Putting your text in graphics because you liked the font better? Naughty naughty. Linking pages with JavaScript? No no no.

If Google cannot read your content or follow your links, then your site is not going to fulfil its potential. If you really need to use images as links, put an alt tag on them, or better still, use CSS so they are written as text links but look like image links.

3. **Flash! Ah ahhh!**
   Flash animations can be really nice, and were quite a common site until recently. Steve Jobs effectively put the nail in the flash coffin by refusing to allow it on apple devices. Google isn't keen on flash either because it's difficult to read any content in there. So best advice is abandon flash now. If you want nice animation effects, html5 can do quite a lot now, and many more browsers support it.

4. **Google Loves BBWs – Big Beautiful Websites**
   Skinny models adorn the home page of fashion websites, but Google, like real men, prefer something with more curves. The bigger your website is, the sexier it is in Google's eyes. If you have a web page with only a couple of sentences on it, this could be seen by Google as low quality and you could be penalised for it. Having lovely fat, chunky paragraphs of rich keyword themed content makes Google go mmmmmm. So if your website is anorexic, consider feeding it up with

more rich content so it gets all fat and juicy. Beware of using artificial padding though. If it reads like you have stuffed your content with fluff, then not only will it be less likely that people will like (and hopefully share) your page, but also more likely that Google will downgrade it.

5. **SEO is 1% inspiration and 99% perspiration**
   Ok so Thomas Edison was talking about Genius when he originally coined the phrase in 1903, but the same principles apply. If anyone tells you they can get you to the top of Google in a couple of weeks, don't believe them. Getting high rankings involves a lot of time and effort. This is why reputable SEO companies don't come cheap. Sure, you can throw money at an Indian SEO company, but more than likely you'll never to see any difference in your rankings.

   Doing SEO is sometimes compared to having a baby (usually by men who have never experienced childbirth, but that's a separate issue). The hardest part is the first few months. After that, things get easier.

   In SEO, the initial on-site work - Checking links are all working, checking content and spelling, updating metatags, doing keyword research and competitor analysis - all takes the greatest time and effort. Once you've done the initial work, things get easier.

3.2 Metatags – what they are and how to use them

A web page is basically a text file. This text file contains little bits of code that tell search engines how to display your content. These bits of code are called 'tags' and are characterised by a left angle bracket '<' at the start and a right angle bracket '>' at the end. A simple example of a tag is:

```
<b>this text is bold</b>
```

The <b> tag tells your browser that whatever comes between the opening <b> and closing </b> tags should be shown in bold (not all tags require closing tags as we'll see later). Other tags include <u> for underline or <i> for italic. Easy really isn't it?

Tags can have nested tags inside them like this:

```
<b>This is Bold <i> and this is bold
italic</i></b>
```

There are other html tags that define the structure of the web page. All web pages should start with a <html> tag and end with a closing </html>tag. This root html tag is should only have 2 different tags directly inside it. This is the <head></head> and the <body></body> tags. (In the latest HTML5 specification the html, head and body tags are optional but it is recommended that you use them to help search engines spider your content).

Inside the <body> tag is all the stuff that you see on the webpage. Inside the <head> tag is all the stuff that is not displayed in your browser but is a container for information about the web page and how the page is displayed - and also a few other things like stylesheets and JavaScript (which we will cover later in Advanced SEO).

For basic SEO, the most important tags are the meta tags. If you go to a website and right click on it, and select 'view source' you'll see something like this:

```
<!DOCTYPE html>
<html lang="en-us">
<head>
<meta charset="utf-8">
<title>W3Schools Online Web Tutorials</title>
<link rel="icon" href="favicon.ico" type="image/x-icon">
<meta name="Keywords" content="HTML, CSS, DOM, JavaScript, jQuery, XML, AJAX, ASP.NET, W3C…">
<meta name="Description" content="HTML CSS JavaScript jQuery AJAX XML ASP.NET SQL Tutorials References Examples">
<meta name="viewport" content="width=device-width">
… ….
```

(This code was taken from w3schools.com.)

The Metatags are all those tags that start with "<meta" The ones used in the example page above are:

- **Charset** – tells the browser what character encoding to use- utf-8 is Unicode character sets. Different languages use different character sets.
- **Keywords** – the meta keywords tells search engines which keywords to use when finding the site
- **Description** – a brief summary of the page
- **Viewport** – tells mobile devices how to present the web page, in this case, stretch to full screen width
- **Title tag** – the title of the web page

The only metatags that are essential to have for SEO is the meta description, and the page title.

Meta Keywords

Google stopped using the meta keywords tag a long time ago because it was abused by spammers who used to stuff it with hundreds of keywords to try to fool Google. That's not to say they ignore it altogether now. If you add lots of content to the meta keywords tag, you might find yourself getting downgraded or possibly even blacklisted for it.

Meta Description

You know that bit of text that appears beneath the links in the Google SERPs, well most of the time (but not always) that text is directly copied from the meta description tag. A good meta description will include keyword related words and should be less than 160 characters in length (Google's search pages cut off text after around 160 characters). I say around 160, but the actual limit is more related to the physical width of the characters, so a meta description with lots of l's in it takes up less space than one with lots of w's in it, and therefore has a greater number of characters before it gets cut.

One recent trend that we are beginning to see now is that for mobile search, the meta description is cut off around 115 characters, and this is also starting to filter into desktop search. Therefore, you should write a shorter and more concise meta description, and aim for around 110 characters to be safe. If you *have* to go over this limit, make sure you don't go further than 160.

The content of the meta description should be natural English readable text. If you put in 'buy bikes, great bikes, road bikes, bikes for tykes, bike buying, bike advice, bike help, bikes by Myke' not only will this signal to Google that the page is spammy, but it will also impact on the number of people who click on your link in the search results. After all, getting people to click through to your site is the ultimate aim of SEO.

A better description would be something like 'Buying your first road bike – from frame size to tyre type, our buying guide will help you choose the perfect ride'. This meta description includes the keywords of 'advice' 'bike' 'guide' and related words 'frame' 'tyre', 'ride' which are all grouped around the keyword theme of bikes and advice.

Page Title

The page title is one of the 10 most important aspects of your webpage. Therefore, it is imperative that you get it right. Your title should be unique to every page on your site. You can use Google Webmaster Tools (GWT) to check if this is the case - GWT is explained in the next chapter 'Advanced SEO' so don't worry if you haven't come across Google Webmaster Tools yet.

To get the perfect page title, you need to try to view your website from your audience's perspective. A title should be short, but describe the primary focus of the page. Let's say for example you have an online shop selling bikes. Your home page title should probably be the title of your business – "myke's bikes – online bike shop" and other pages in your site should be equally succinct. For example the shipping and returns policy page title should simply be 'Shipping and returns'. Note you should not try to stuff the keywords in your page title unless it is appropriate they be there. If it is appropriate, try to put the keywords near the start of the title tag.

The length of your page title should be less than 55 characters. This length would be visible in 512 pixel width displays, and be quite easy to embed in limited character tweets. Only the first 20-25 character are visible in browser tabs so it's worth considering that when creating page titles.

Note, the title that appears in Google's search results are not necessarily guaranteed to be the ones that you selected for your page. Sometimes, Google works in mysterious ways.

3.3 Backlinks – the right and wrong way to do them

If a website links back to your website, that's what is known as a 'backlink' - obvious really. The number of backlinks is probably less important than the quality of these links. In early SEO, you could get great success by creating thousands of automated backlinks from spamming blog sites and link exchange systems. Now such practices are frowned upon and backlink spamming is more likely to get your site penalised than help it.

There are a number of factors that determine how good a backlink is. Some of these are:

1. Popularity – a page that has lots of backlinks to it gives higher quality backlinks itself.
2. Topic relevant – if a page is themed on a similar topic or keyword cluster to yours, then it will have higher quality. Backlinks from irrelevant pages are generally considered worthless.
3. Anchor text – not as highly valued as it used to be, but the keywords used to link to your page are relevant. The best backlinks have similar link text to the title tag of your page
4. Trust Rank – this is a score used by search engines to measure how much they trust the website that the link is on. Certain top level domains (TLDs) like .gov and .ac are more highly trusted than regular .coms.
5. Age – fresh links tend to have higher quality than older ones. However, on the flip side, old domain names generally have higher trust rankings. If you can keep links fresh, then your backlinks are more useful.

6. Link neighbourhoods – spammy sites tend to link back to other spammy sites. If you are caught up in a 'bad link neighbourhood' then you will need to take action to get the link removed, or disavow the link in Google Webmaster Tools.

Getting good quality backlinks is all about identifying where your links should be and then getting them there. Social sharing is a good way to make your page known, and some of those people who see your page in social media might add backlinks to them on their own blogs and websites, so having social media sharing buttons is vital.

Another source of backlinks is to write reviews. If you have a product or service you can submit a review on other websites, or you can give away trials and free samples to bloggers and YouTube vloggers to get more back traffic. YouTube will not necessarily give you backlinks, but the whole aim of SEO is to get traffic, not just get your page to the top of a list of pages, so this tactic cuts out the Google middleman.

If you have tried any products, you can write testimonials for people. For the sake of 10 minutes work, you can get your backlink on some high quality sites, and you might even get your picture on there too if you're lucky!

There are many other tactics that you can employ to get backlinks, some are sneaky like finding relevant domains that have recently expired and exploiting their backlinks. Some are legitimate like targeting .edu sites with links/resources pages. And some are just hard work, like writing content for other sites and journalists ('content marketing').

The best way to get good backlinks is to make sure your page is worth linking to. Have unique, good quality, interesting, funny or provocative content that will make people want to bookmark and share. That's the number one way to get great backlinks.

3.4 Robots.txt file

The 'robots.txt' file is a small text file that sits in the root folder of your website. Having a robots.txt file probably won't affect your SEO much but it takes literally seconds to create one and it could influence how search engines see your website. At a bare minimum, a robots.txt file should include the following:

```
User-agent: *
Allow: /
```

This entry tells all search engines that they are allowed to index every page on your site. You can specify individual spiders to not index certain parts of the website, but the spiders don't have to take this advice so might crawl the whole site anyway. If a spammy spider is scraping the content of your website, telling it which pages it should not crawl will make no difference at all.

The one important thing I would advise is do not reveal any hidden urls in your robots file. I've seen examples where people have used disallow: /admin – which tells spiders not to include a link to your admin folder, but also tells potential hackers where your admin folder is located.

The only time I would advise putting more than the basic minimum into your site is when content is duplicated, e.g. if you have two paths to reach the same url. So in my shop example, I can go to www.mykesbikes.com/newarrivals/shinybike which could show the same content as www.mykesbikes.com/kids-bikes/shinybike .

In this instance I might disallow the /newarrivals folder.
Duplicate content can hurt your rankings but you can add
special metatags called 'canonical URLs' to point Google at the
correct url for the content. Canonical urls are covered later in
chapter 6.2 "Duplicate Content Penalty."

Recently, Google has started indexing search result urls, e.g.
mykekesbikes.com/search.aspx?s=search-keywords If this is
happening, you can disallow the search results pages by
using:

```
User-agent: *
Disallow: /?s=
```

3.5 Sitemaps

There are two types of sitemaps on a website. The html sitemap and the xml sitemap. The HTML sitemap is a list of links in hierarchical form designed to help users navigate complex websites. They also help search engine spiders find parts of your site that might be deeply linked.

The other type of sitemap is an xml file located in the root of your website often called sitemap.xml. The sitemap.xml file is structured in a formal way using the sitemaps.org guidelines and contains a list of your websites pages along with the following information:

1. url of the page
2. date last modified
3. change frequency – always, hourly, daily, weekly, monthly, yearly or never
4. Priority – how important this page is compared to other pages on the site, range is from 0.0 to 1.0. Default priority is 0.5. Homepage should always be set to 1.0

There are plenty of free sitemap generators online if you don't fancy writing it out by hand (who would?). A quick Google should be able to find you one easily. Sitemap generators simply spider your website and generate the xml file for you to download.

Once you have created your sitemap you can submit it to Google webmaster tools, and maybe Bing webmaster tools, although I would not waste too much time on the latter. Most search engines should be able to spider your whole site without needing the sitemap file, and if they can't then there is something wrong with your site linking structure.

3.6 Black hat, Grey hat, and White hat SEO techniques

Google hates SEO. Yes you heard me, Google really, really hates SEO. It believes that all websites should have an equal chance of getting to the top of Google, and those sites which are at the top are the bestest rootin' tootin' sites in the west. Or east depending on your geo location. In a perfect Google world, when you search for 'best cheese in the world' you should get the most authoritative resource dedicated to the world's best cheese, written by the world's leading cheese expert with lots of backlinks from other authoritative cheese websites saying this is the best page for cheese. Ever.

In the real world, competition for the top spots is fierce. For some keywords, the difference between position 1 and position 2 could mean millions of dollars worth of business, so the attraction of SEO is huge. Google realise this, and imposes 'webmaster guidelines' (https://support.Google.com/webmasters/answer/35769?hl=e n) designed to make sure that website owners are on their best behaviour. The guidelines fall into 3 areas:

1. **Content and design guidelines** – rules about how your site should be organised, and structured. Using text instead of images, having a reasonable number of links, have descripting <title> elements, no broken links etc.

2. **Technical guidelines** – covers site loading speed, use robots.txt, making site appear correctly in different browser and mobile devices and a few other technical bits and bobs.

3. **Quality guidelines** – do not copy content from other websites, do not include keyword stuffing or spammy text, do not use cloaking, hidden text or doorway pages (see black hat SEO below)

Any deviation from the guidelines means your website is looked upon more suspiciously by Google. In a worst case scenario you could find your site blacklisted. And when that happens it's a right pain to get it back in the index to the position it was in before the penalty.

White Hat SEO
The terms 'white hat' and 'black hat' come from the old black and white westerns where the hero sheriff always wore a white hat, and the bad guys always wore black hats. So anyone who practices 'White hat' SEO is someone who abides by all the rules of the webmaster guidelines and who doesn't try to use tricks or sneaky tactics to manipulate their search engine rankings.

Good white hat SEO focuses on the content and accessibility of the website, making sure that the content is as rich and useful as possible, while at the same time making it easy as possible for people to find and read the information there.

Interestingly, what Google decides as white hat or black hat is influenced by how much it trusts your website. An authoritative website with a high trust rank can get away with more than a fresh new website with few backlinks.

Black Hat SEO

What is considered Black Hat now was almost certainly allowed in the old wild-west days of the internet. When there were few rules and SEO cowboys reaped the rewards. Over time, these practices have become outlawed and breaking the rules can land you in Google prison (metaphorically speaking of course). There are cases where the CEO of black hat SEO companies have actually been sent to prison. Matt Marlon who ran an infamous black hat SEO firm Traffic Power was sent to prison in 2008. Turns out the sort of companies that employ black hat tactics are also the sort of companies that runs other fraudulent scams.

So what types of activities are likely to land you in trouble? Well, here's a few of them:

1. Hidden text on pages – hiding text on a page using HTML comments or using CSS or layering other content over the top. In today's html5 rich environment, it's difficult to say when text in hidden. For example, in a pure CSS drop down menu, the sub menu links are initially hidden on the page until you mouseover the parent menu item.

2. Cloaking and redirects – if your website redirects visitors to a different version of the site from the one that Google sees, then you can optimise the Google version of the site for specific keywords while making the non-Google version of the site show different content. Sometimes the different content is displayed on the same page. This method is called 'cloaking'. Sometimes you might want to use redirects based on IP address, e.g. to deliver local content. In this instance it's

better to present a link to that page, or better still, optimise a different webpage for the local content.

3. Keyword stuffing – repeating the same keyword too many times in your content – in title tags, in link tags, alt tags, everywhere. This is relatively easy to avoid if you are writing content in normal everyday language. *But if your keyword-stuffed text and keywords are really stuffed with lots of keywords and stuff then the keyword here is don't stuff your keywords with stuff.* See what I mean? Reading spammy stuffed content is difficult to understand and is difficult to do accidentally.

4. Doorway pages – this is different from landing pages. A landing page is a page specifically designed to be a destination for a marketing message. For example, an email containing links to a special offer might go to a special landing page which has call to actions and more information. A doorway page is simply there to funnel traffic through to another page via a high Google ranking. This type of page would be focused on a specific keyword, e.g. 'shiny kid's bikes for 6 year old'. And then the black hat person would create more doorway pages, e.g. 'shiny children's bikes for 7 year olds'. With each focused doorway page, you could potentially funnel a lot of traffic.

Often, doorway pages would be keyword stuffed and contain hidden content, spammy backlinks and custom JavaScript redirections to the main website which would not redirect search engine spiders, just normal web visitors.

5. Content swapping – this occurs when a page is optimised for a certain keyword, e.g. 'men's health' and then after it is indexed for this phrase, the content is changed to something else e.g. 'Viagra pills'. Often redirections or hidden text are used so the search engines still think the page is about 'men's health'. Google spiders are very clever though. They check your site using different 'user agents' some of them simulate real web browsers so if your content looks different to different spiders, then you are going to get found out. And banned.

6. Parasite content – If a hacker can place a webpage on a trusted domain then any links from this web page will have higher value. The page itself will also benefit from higher rankings. Generally if the parasite page is on a different subject to the main site, this will flag warnings in Google's systems. A couple of years ago, there was a lot of link injection attacks after an exploit on WordPress was found. The spammers managed to place links into the victim's site databases which made the parasitic links appear on existing web pages and in existing content. This attack affected many thousands of WordPress websites before it was patched.

7. Google Bombing – this involves creating software to automate the process of creating links on other websites. It's relatively easy to create automated backlinks on blogs and other types of user generated

content sites. If you create millions of backlinks in a few days, this would help rankings very briefly, but damage your website greatly. This tactic can also be used for negative SEO which is covered in chapter 7.

8. Paid links – a big fat NO-NO in Google is paying people to put links back to your site. However if you make a donation to a charity or a kickstarter project and they put a link back to you saying that you support their cause, then this is ok.

9. Duplicate content – copying someone else's content and meta tags to get high rankings. If the page is already indexed by Google, then your site will be flagged as a copy and your content will not appear in Google at all.

10. Link farming – put lots of back links on lots of link farms and spammy link directories and you will be punished. You have been warned!

11. Map spamming – pretending to have offices local to different locations then registering these on Google maps.

12. Domain grabbing – buying up expired domains just for the sake of taking advantage of their backlinks.

13. Article spinning – involves getting a few articles from other sites on a particular topic, mashing bits of them together and posing as unique content on your site. You can also use this method to submit articles to other

sites.

14. Optimised anchors – use the same keyword targeted anchor text for all your backlinks used to be a powerful tactic. Now it is deemed black hat. Instead you should use more varied text or better still the URL of the page.

15. Social media spam – a relatively new thing but you can get companies offering you hundreds of twitter followers and shares or hundreds of Facebook shares. These tools work by creating spam social media accounts and automating the process of sharing content. Some Indian companies actually hire hundreds of low paid workers to create fake accounts to bypass the security restrictions on Facebook and twitter, and then sell followers and shares to companies for a few pence per account. This is not officially black hat yet, so can probably be counted as grey hat...

Grey Hat SEO

Somewhere between black hat and white hat is the murky grey area. Grey Hat SEO is the practice of using technically legal methods to improve your site rankings, but which are ethically dubious, and could one day become black hat. Think of it like legal highs. They might be legal today and get you high, but in a couple of years' time you could get punished for using them when the law changes to catch up with the new compounds.

It's very easy to use Black Hat SEO and get found out. It's a bit harder to get caught using grey hat SEO for example, it's difficult sometimes for Google to know whether you have paid for links.

Grey hat SEO involves much more creativity than Black hat SEO. The reason Grey hat SEO is less known about is that as soon as the search engines become aware that people are using these techniques, they take steps to prevent them, which turns a grey hat technique into a black hat technique.

At the risk of exposing Grey hat SEO here is a list of some of the things that are technically legal, but outside the realms of white hat SEO:

1. SEO Squatting: buy up expired domains which are relevant to your keywords and then add some pages of content with a few well-placed backlinks to your site. Make sure that the new content is good quality and not too different from what the website hosted before. Put some AdWords on the new content and then do some satellite SEO on it to keep up its trust rank.

2. Create Social media accounts for your pets. Really this works. Get some cute stories and pictures, then one day

your pet suddenly develops an interest in power tools, or mobility aids, or whatever website you are trying to promote. This will then create social search links back to your website. Not against Google's rules to do this, but could contravene the social media that it is hosted on. Then again, who's going to sue a dog?

3. Redesign your website at regular intervals - even if the content is more or less the same, because the code and text changes, Google thinks that this is fresh content.

4. Add a comments box to your site pages and invite anyone to comment. Sure it could get you 9 million spammers to put their links on there, but if you only approve the less spammy ones and then replace their links with a rel=nofollow tag, this means that you get no backlinks bleeding your page rank, but what you do get is lots of fresh content with hopefully relevant text for no effort on your part.

5. Link yourself higher. Whenever you put a comment on any blog, always make an excuse to link back to yourself. While you're at it, get into the habit of being very helpful. Join forums where you can post solutions to other people's problems. Moneysavingexpert.com is a great one as it gets lots of traffic and has a plethora of relevant topics.

6. Use those sharing buttons unashamedly - add Facebook like and tweet this buttons everywhere you can. Then click on them yourself a few times. Get your dog to

click on them too (see tip 2 above). You could even add google+ too but they will just sit at the footer on your site gathering dust unless you click on them yourself.

7. This is a really sneaky one- set up a targeted paid directory specialising in one field - e.g. if you are trying to promote power tools, call it a 'power tools review website'. Then add all your competitors to the directory. Add some content over the next few weeks, then after a few weeks, change the website to say that all links on the site require a $199 inclusion fee, and then report all the competitor sites on the directory as paying for links. This is an example of negative SEO which is difficult to ban you for.

8. Use the free AdWords vouchers that you get in computer magazines. Every month I get PC Pro magazine and every month it has a £50 AdWords voucher in it. Generally I set up new temporary AdWords accounts, whack in the 50 quid code and set them going. Bosh. Easy traffic for free.

9. Fabricate news – news websites are desperate for content, and quite a few of them have very lax authentication procedures. If you can fabricate some news and maybe get yourself a few backlinks or twitter shares on the back of it, then you can potentially get a lot of traffic.

10. Charity links. Select a few relevant small charities, make a small donation and write an article about the

good work that they do with a link to their donation page and then ask them to link back to you as thanks: paid links but without the Google penalty.

11. Use Negative SEO - this is a collection of techniques which you can find out more about in the Negative SEO. Essentially this is forcing other websites above you down in the rankings to help your own ranking. There are 11 techniques on this page:

- Removal requests
- Promote non offending content - "Insulation"
- Google Bowling
- Site Infection
- Tattling
- Guilty by Association
- False duplicated content
- Denial of Service Attacks (DOS)
- Click Fraud
- AdSense Banning
- Black social bookmarking

12. Read the relevant chapter on Negative SEO for more details on these tactics.

13. Use Keyword Association Manipulation - this is when you associate two unrelated keywords together to try to fool bots into thinking that they are semantically related or synonymous. This is quite an advanced technique and takes a lot of work to achieve on highly competitive keywords.

14. Use a subscription based service to hide non relevant content - a bit like cloaking, you are showing different content to spiders, but if you have a subscription based service - even if it's just a 'click here to prove you are over 12 years old' button, you can get away with having one set of content for spiders (and people who claim to be under 12 - in which case they would get a less interesting set of pages about the joys of power tools) and another set for most other people.

15. Pay another site to put the Google authentication html file on their website. Then add the site to Google webmaster tools and use the 'change of address' tool to redirect linkjuice back to your website. This is not paying for links because there are no direct links that go back to your site which are paid for, so you are just paying for the link juice. The webmaster that you are paying will be aware that this is what you are doing and if they agree to it, it's not against the webmaster guidelines (yet).

16. Spun Content - this is copying content from another site but changing some words around so search engines cannot automatically spot the plagiarism. Another method is to take content from more than one page. As they say, copying from one source is plagiarism, copying from more than one source is research. A good way to do this is to use lists like "Top 10 SEO Techniques" then steal some items from other peoples lists and compile your own. If you add a few extra ideas in, it becomes your own work. See how I recopied

this paragraph from the black hat SEO section above?

17. Write negative reviews - when people are researching products or services they are much more likely to read negative reviews than positive ones so they know what to look out for.

18. Link chaining - In the old days of the world wide web, before search engines became ubiquitous, there were a lot of 'web rings' - these are sites that join a group or 'web ring' and each site puts a bit of JavaScript code on their page. The web ring hub site would then write links into this code so that each website in the ring had links to the next one. In this way you could cycle between all the sites in the ring. Link chaining is a similar method whereby you create rings of sites and each links to the next one in the ring. None of the sites themselves have more than one chained link and they all have different IP addresses, so cannot be associated as a 'bad neighbourhood'

19. Pay for reviews - there are plenty of people out there who write reviews on websites in exchange for money. The blog-whores will write about any old subject as long as they are getting paid, and this is perfectly legal.

20. Free Stuff! Everyone likes getting something for free, so why not put voucher codes for relevant products on your site. You can get plenty of codes from online voucher code websites (Just Google 'voucher codes') and pop a 'voucher of the day' feature on your website.

Technically this is not plagiarism or duplicated content, and if you push this feature on twitter, Facebook etc. you'll attract lots of traffic.

21. Content repositioning – You won't find this tactic on the web, because I invented it. The premise is thus: most people only read the first few sentences on a page before they lose interest. Therefore, having call to action at the top of the page is very handy. On the downside, the more keyword themed content which is better for search engines is less likely to grab someone's attention. Therefore, you should move your content on the page itself so the SEO friendly stuff but lower conversion text is at the top of the code, but bottom of the page. This can be achieved by various means such as using CSS floats, CSS absolute positioning, jQuery append() methods or similar. You can also create jQuery animations to change content position, or possibly ajax to insert content. All of which is technically allowed (for now).

For balance, it must be pointed out that the concept of Grey hat SEO is a contentious issue. Some people believe that Grey Hat SEO is just a less obvious form of Black Hat SEO, and some argue that there's no such thing as Grey Hat SEO, just lucky people who get away with it for a while.

3.7 Creating great quality content

One of the recurring mantras of SEO is 'Content is King'. This has never been as true as it is today with more emphasis being placed on the content of your website than the backlinks and metatags.

Latent Semantic Indexing
 Google uses a variety of measures to determine how good your web content is. One of the ways is to use a mathematical technique called **Latent Semantic Indexing (LSI)**. Essentially, LSI uses natural language processing on the copy of a web page to try to determine the topic or 'theme' of the page. Using LSI, themes and patterns of word relationships are generated. For example, if the word 'mother' appears with the word 'child' then often, then these two concepts are linked. The strength of that relationship is determined by the relative frequency in which these words appear. Also, the distance between the words in the text is important. Although the word 'semantic' is used, this method of classifying content does not mean that the computer knows the meaning of the text.

When a searcher types a keyword into Google, the keyword is evaluated to see how closely related it is to the pages in the index, and this relativity score is used as a factor for ranking pages.

It's all a bit complicated and mysterious really, but if you want to get high rankings in Google for a given keyword, then you need to know which other words are associated with it, and include these in your web page content. This process is actually easier than it sounds. Basically, all you have to do is get a list of maybe a dozen pages that Google thinks are a good match for this keyword, and then extract the more common words from these pages that you think are related to the theme.

Keyword generation
So how do you get a list of semantically related web pages? Simple! Use Google search. The top ten pages in your search results are the ones that are Google think are more closely related to the search topic, and helpfully provides you with these pages that you need to gather. Once you have the closely related content, you can then generate your own content using the keyword themes that the top pages use. Note, using keyword themes does not mean writing the same keyword several times in your page. Often, the top ranking pages for a keyword might only include the keyword once or twice, or even not at all, but the other content of the page is deemed sufficiently close to the theme to give it high ranking.

The process of copying and pasting text from high ranking pages is a real chore to do manually. Fortunately there are SEO tools that can do this for you. The best one I have found is Ultimate Keyword Hunter by appselorometer. You can download it for free from here:
http://ultimatekeywordhunter.com/.

To use UKH, download the software and when you open it, you will see a screen like this:

Type in your keyword in the box and select the number of pages to compare. I use 20 normally, but 10 is usually sufficient.

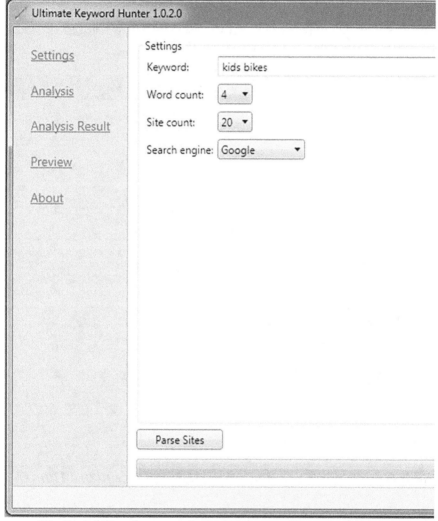

Fig 5: Adding keywords in Ultimate Keyword Hunter

Click on 'parse sites' and the software will read the top results in Google for your keyword. Note, Google uses your location to generate search results, so if you are in the UK, you will get more UK sites at the top, and if you are in the US then you are more likely to get US websites.

After the program has finished parsing the sites, click on 'analysis' in the left menu and it will show you the list of web pages that Google provided:

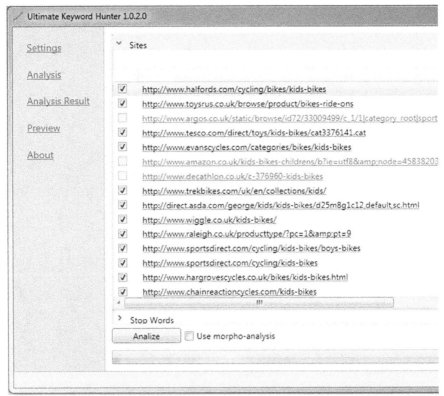

Fig 6: List of sites to analyse in Ultimate Keyword Hunter

Sometimes the pages that Google returns could not be parsed, for example if they return 404 page not found errors, so you cannot select the checkbox for these sites. If there are any pages returned which appear to be irrelevant you can deselect them by clicking on the checkbox next to them. Once you have selected the sites you want to analyse, click on the 'Analize' [sic] button. This will then tell the program to spider all the selected pages and get the most common words used in each page.

The 'stop words' link just above the analize button allows you to modify the list of words that will not be used in the analysis. Common works like 'and', 'is', and 'are' should be excluded as they are not useful content words. The program comes prepopulated with a pretty good list of stop words out of the box so you should not need to modify them.

Once the process of collecting the content is completed, a message box will appear saying 'analysis complete'. You can then click on 'Analysis Result' to see what words were found.

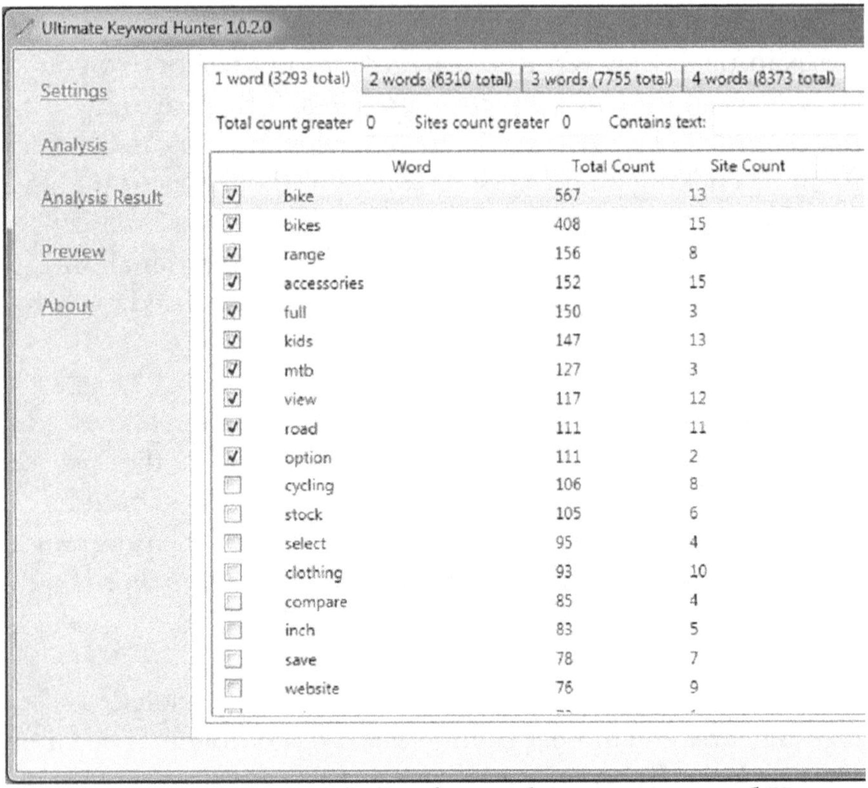

Fig 7: *Retrieved keywords list from Ultimate Keyword Hunter*

The analysis shows that, unsurprisingly, the most common word used on these pages is 'bike'. However, it also shows a list of other keywords that you might not have thought of such as 'road' and 'clothing'. These words are likely to be semantically related in Google's index so is useful to include. Single keywords are handy, but when you look at the 2 and 3 word phrases, these tend to be powerful theme words.

In the example below, it looks like we might have accidentally spidered a French language website, so these keywords can probably be disregarded:

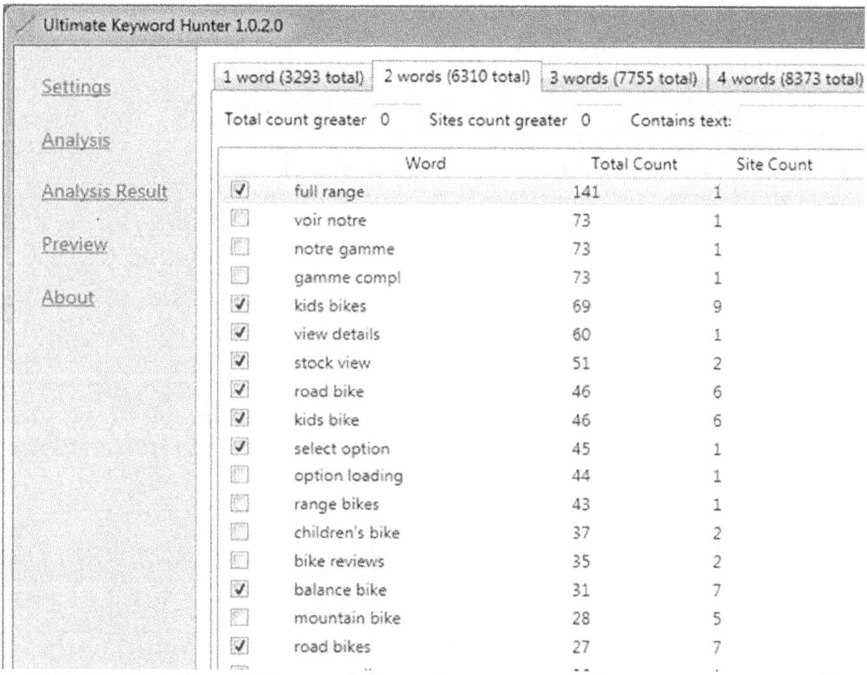

Ultimate Keyword Hunter 1.0.2.0			
	1 word (3293 total)	2 words (6310 total)	3 words (7755 total)	4 words (8373 total)

Settings

Analysis

Total count greater 0   Sites count greater 0   Contains text:

	Word	Total Count	Site Count
✓	full range	141	1
	voir notre	73	1
	notre gamme	73	1
	gamme compl	73	1
✓	kids bikes	69	9
✓	view details	60	1
✓	stock view	51	2
✓	road bike	46	6
✓	kids bike	46	6
✓	select option	45	1
	option loading	44	1
	range bikes	43	1
	children's bike	37	2
	bike reviews	35	2
✓	balance bike	31	7
	mountain bike	28	5
✓	road bikes	27	7

Analysis Result

Preview

About

Fig 8: Retrieved 2 word key phrases in Ultimate Keyword Hunter

Now that we have a good list of themed keywords to use in our content, we can probably generate some quite rich text. And UKH will help us do this too! Click on 'Preview' in the left hand side and you will see a screen something like this:

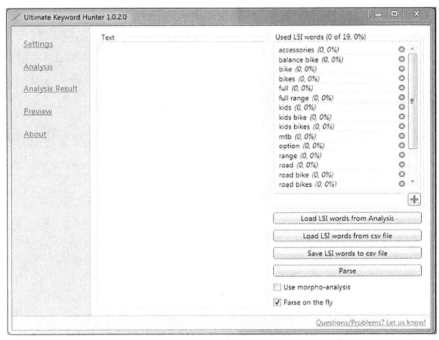

Fig 9: Generating rich text in Ultimate Keyword Hunter using LSI word list

Click on 'load LSI words from Analysis' and this will populate the keywords list on the right hand side, listed in order of occurrence (and by implication, semantic relevance).

Now you can type the content of your page in the middle text box and each time you use a keyword from the left hand side, it is indicated by a strike-through style and the percentage of used words at the top increases.

In this example, I've just used the keywords to generate some generic text, focussing more on the keywords at the top:

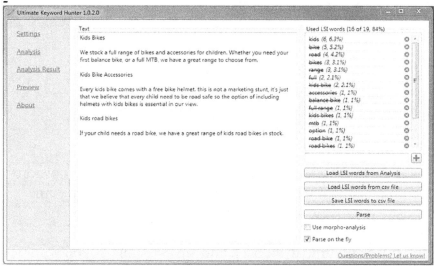

Fig 10 –Rich text generated using Ultimate Keyword Hunter

Reading back through the generated text, it sounds like I know what I am talking about! But I'm just making up sentences using the keywords provided.

Using this method of creating content is a very powerful way to getting good rankings in Google. With a bit of practice, you can be a great content writer in a very short space of time.

Chapter 4 – Advanced SEO

4.1 Mastering Advanced SEO Techniques

If you have read all of section 3 – well done! You are now an SEO Blue belt! You have enough training to promote your website in Google and call yourself an SEO warrior.

But, this is no time to sit back and sip cocktails. If you want to succeed in this highly competitive business, then you must learn to mater the more advanced SEO techniques and become an SEO ninja...

4.2 Long Tail Keywords

The first Advanced SEO skill you should learn is mastery of Long Tailed Keywords.

What are Long Tail Keywords in SEO?

Long tail keywords are often misunderstood by SEO practitioners. Many people incorrectly believe them to be longer key phrases with more words them. This is wrong. A long tail keyword is a keyword (or more accurately key phrase) which is rarely used in search engines and therefore has low traffic. Examples of which are 'Cleethorpes web design', 'SEO Lincolnshire', 'weight loss surgery in Manchester' or 'flame patterned contact lenses'. A related concept is 'niche marketing' which is covered later in this book.

The moniker 'long tail' comes from a statistical concept called the 'normal distribution'. A normal distribution is a recurring phenomenon that appears throughout nature. A prosaic example follows: imagine you question 100 women at random and ask them how many pairs of shoes they own. You will probably see a frequency graph something like this:

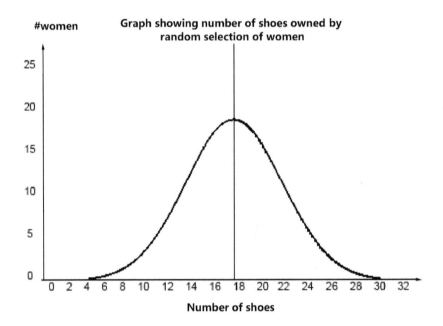

Fig 11: normal distribution curve example

As you can see, most people are gathered around the centre value (the mean) and fewer people appear at the extreme end of the graph.

The outlying values at the extreme end are called the 'tails', and in SEO the concept of long tail means the infrequently searched key phrases that, if plotted on a frequency graph, would appear towards the outlying ends of the frequency distribution.

Take the following example:

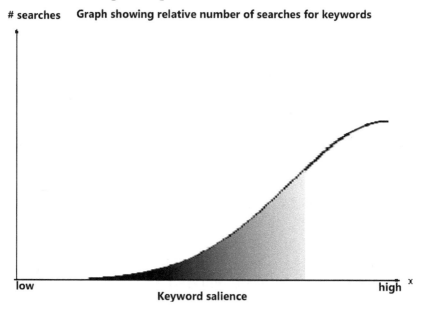

Fig 12: Long tail of normal distribution for keyword salience

This graph shows the relation between the frequency (or salience) of a phrase and the number of searches done in a search engine, note that this is a one tailed normal distribution. This is a simplified explanation so the actual graph would be slightly different.

As you can see on the graph, the shaded area represents the search frequency for low volume searches. In this case, the low volume searches approximates to about half of the volume of the graph. Therefore, the number of long tail keyword searches for this result would be 50% of the overall search traffic.

For a more detailed treatment of the normal distribution see this page: http://en.wikipedia.org/wiki/Normal_distribution .

Why are long tail keywords important?

Some SEO experts claim that up to 80% of search traffic can come from long tail keywords. Personally I believe this to be a great over-exaggeration, and in some cases, can be used as an excuse to appease clients when their high frequency, targeted keywords do less well in the search engine rankings results. The actual figure depends on where you draw the division between long tail keyword and high frequency keywords, and on what shape your traffic curve is. It also depends on how competitive your targeted keyword is. If you target a page at the keyword 'software' you will find it very difficult to get to the first few pages of Google, but if you target the keywords 'enquires management software' that would be much easier to get to the first page in the SERPs. Therefore, focussing on long tail keywords, especially at the start of a new SEO campaign is a good idea for drawing early traffic.

Another reason for looking at long tail keywords is the conversion rates. Specific keyword searches tend to have much higher conversion rates, for example, if you are a shop in Cleethorpes selling men's clothing, then you will have a much higher conversion rate for 'Cleethorpes menswear' than you would for 'men's clothing' - even if you were on the first page of Google for both phrases.

Should you optimise for Long Tail Keywords in Search Engines?

This is a difficult question to answer, and depends greatly on the type of site you are promoting, and the budget. If your site is niche or your budget is small, then definitely, your focus should be on the long tail keywords which are more relevant to your site, and will get you better quality traffic. If you are promoting a site in a competitive market, and your SEO budget is good enough, then you are better off optimising for more competitive keywords, and then using AdWords for the long tail keywords, which will be relatively cheaper. You will find that when optimising for the competitive keywords, a good proportion of search engine referrals will come from long tail keywords anyway, although if you are doing your job properly, your ratio of long tail keywords should not be anywhere near 80%.

4.3 SEO Zooming

What is SEO Zooming?

SEO Zooming is an advanced SEO technique that Blackbox invented which involves gradually changing the focus of the SEO from the most specific, long tail keywords to the more generic, higher traffic keywords.

Take the following example: if I wanted to use the SEO Zooming technique to promote our website **Blackbox E-Marketing** for the keywords '**Medical Marketing**_' - the first thing I would need to do is identify how competitive the keyword is. A quick glance at Google will tell you that there are 87.2 million results. Here I'm using Google.co.uk to find the competition rate, not Google.com. The reason for this is that our clients are all based in the UK. There's no point trying to get good rankings in search engines which are tailored for countries in which you do not normally do business. (There are exceptions to this, but adaptation of your core business model is outside the scope of this book).

Ok, having established that you are up against 87 million different web pages for this keyword, you can pretty much guarantee that you are not going to get to page 1 of Google very easily. Therefore we need to zoom in our SEO efforts to something more achievable. The next step is to develop a hierarchy of semantic terms. Consider the following diagram:

Fig 13: Example hierarchy of semantically related terms for medical marketing

How do we find the other phrases? Well, Google helpfully provides us with related phrases when you type in your search term, at the bottom it says 'Searches related to X' and using this information we can plot a hierarchy and semantically related phrases using Google's own algorithm! (You don't have to use Google's related keywords to generate this map, you can use your own)

For each step, we enter the search term, select the most appropriate and more specific related keyword, then drill down to that one, and select the next step.

In this example, the hierarchy is not great, so instead I use the geographic filter and make the second level of zoom to be UK Medical Marketing. Now we're down to 19 million results. Another trick to find the next level of zoom is to add elements to the phrase, so the next step we're going to use is '**uk medical marketing and medical websites**' - now we're down to a manageable 2 million results. And if you look in Google, **www.blackboxemarketing.com** is already ranked number 1 for that phrase, brilliant, now we can zoom out the SEO to the next level which is **UK Medical Marketing** - our site is ranked number 3 for this particular search phrase. Not too bad. At this point we can either focus the SEO at this level, or zoom out again. The decision on whether to focus or zoom out depends on a number of factors, but the two most important questions are:

1. Will higher rankings for this search term get me significantly more traffic?

2. Will zooming out have a negative impact on the conversion rates?

This has to be decided on a case by case basis and there are no hard and fast rules for this.

In this example, the decision has been made to go to the next step, which happens to be the first node in our hierarchy - Medical Marketing. After a few months of SEO, we are now ranked number 6 in Google. This is probably a good time to focus on the medical marketing keyword and try to get higher rankings for this.

What do you do after SEO Zooming is successful?

So, you've got to the top for your primary search phrase? Well the next step is to do a sideways shift. This is what I call **SEO Panning.** The way this works is to get good rankings for a very closely related SEO phrase. This technique differs from SEO zooming in that the focus of panning is to get more and better conversions, not necessarily more traffic.

4.4 Canonical URLs

A website can sometimes contain the same text on different variations of the page. This can be for a number of reasons. Sometimes the same article is posted in a different directory on the same website so could have urls like '/articles/bikes/buying-guide' and '/articles/tips/buying-guide'. Other times it could be because the website has aliases, e.g. 'mykesbikes.co.uk/articles/buying-guide' and mykesbikes.com/articles/buying-guide'.

If your website publishes the same content in different urls, then Google may not automatically select the correct URL. If Google sees the same content in a different URL, then your site might be downgraded with a duplicate content penalty, or may be judged as less authoritative.

How do you make sure Google uses the correct URL?

There are a few methods you can use:

1. **Be consistent with the URL across your website.**
   And if you can, use absolute links if your website has aliased urls (including sites where you have both www and non www versions of your address that show the same content, or http and https versions that are the same)

2. **Use redirects for non-primary urls.**
   If you can put 301 redirects on duplicate content pages then this tells Google not to index the incorrect version. It will also help if you have backlinks to the wrong url

3. **Use a rel=canonical link element tag.**
   In the <head> element of your web page, you can add a special html tag that looks a bit like this:

   ```
   <link rel="canonical"
   href="http://mykebikes.com/articles/buying-
   guide" />
   ```

   Search engines will then see this link and know that the preferred URL for the page should be the one indicated. Be warned though, if you mistype the URL in the canonical tag, then your page could be excluded from Google.

4. **Use Google webmaster tools to set preferred domain.**
   this works with aliased domains but not with different folder structures

5. **Use a sitemap to indicate preference.**
   XML Sitemaps include full urls of the page, so having the canonical URL in the sitemap may be beneficial. This is not as powerful a method as using rel=canonical tags though as sometimes the sitemap information might not considered when deciding preferred urls.

6. **Specify the canonical link in the HTTP Headers.**
   This is a more technical procedure and you will need to have access to your web server to configure the http headers. Each type of web server has a different method of adding http headers so I won't go into detail

how to do it here, but if you know how to do it, the header should look something like this:

```
Link: <http://mykebikes.com/articles/buying-
guide >; rel="canonical"
```

4.5 NoFollow Link Attributes

Remember the diagram in Section 2.3 above? The way link juice is distributed amongst web pages depends on how many links come in to your page and how many links go out of your web page. If you have lots of outgoing links, then your page value will decrease as all the juice leaks out. You can prevent this by using 'nofollow' attributes in your link tags. Nofollow links look a bit like this:

```
<a href="http://mykesbikes.com" rel="nofollow">
```

Originally, nofollow links were intended to instruct search engine spiders not to follow the link on the page and spider it, but since the generation 2 search engines, these nofollow links are also used to modify the SEO effect of having outward bound links.

Generally, the rule should be, if the outbound link goes to any site which you don't own, then you should use rel=nofollow. No follow links can also be applied to internal links on a website. This allows site owners to do something called 'link sculpting'.

Link Sculpting

Link sculpting is a technique used to manipulate the rankings of pages using nofollow attributes for certain links. For example, if you wanted to emphasise a single page on your website such as the contact page, but was less concerned about your home page, then in the navigation of your website you could add nofollow links to all the pages of the site apart from the contact page. This would then mean that more link juice would be channelled into your contact page but none to your other pages.

Link sculpting is a fine art, and can be a powerful method of promoting a single landing page or featured product. Sometimes it's better to have one page at rank 1 than 100 pages at rank 30 for different keywords. However, Link sculpting as a strategy is not generally recommended as search engine spiders might ignore pages which have nofollow links on them, which reduces your search engine presence.

4.6 Google Webmaster Tools

This sounds like a superhero's utility belt doesn't it? Batman might have had shark repellent spray in his belt, but SEOman has a GWT box down his shorts.

The Google Webmaster Toolbox is indispensable for SEO experts as it contains some very powerful tools. We'll look at the main tools below:

1. **Sitemap Submission Tool**
   Allows you to point Google at your xml sitemap and instruct it to read the file (see section 3.5 for more info on sitemap files). You can also test whether your sitemap is valid using this tool.

2. **Crawl rate tool**
   Google decides how often to crawl your site. Using this tool you can ask Google to spider your site a bit faster – very handy for websites that are frequently updated

3. **Crawl Errors monitor**
   This little beauty will let you know if Google cannot access any pages of your site for any reason. If your website has been unreachable or some problem with the site itself, CEM will let you know.

4. **Search Queries Tool**
   This lets you know which search queries your site appears in (whether it was clicked on or not) and also lets you know how many searches for that query

appeared in the time period. This is information that is not available anywhere else (not even in Google analytics – see chapter 5)

5. **Mobile Usability Checker**
   A relatively new tool in the box. Since Google started using mobile compatibility as a ranking signal, the mobile usability tool is a very useful bit of kit, especially when you have lots of websites that you need to keep track of.

6. **Backlinks Tool**
   This will give you a sample of links to your site, and what page is linked to and what text is used.

7. **HTML Improvement tool**
   Really handy, will show you which pages are missing title tags, meta description tags and has meta descriptions that are outside the optimal length. You can also use this to identify duplicate title and meta description tags.

8. **Remove URLs tool**
   If you have a problem, if no one else can help, and if you can find them, maybe you can hire the A-Team... Failing that, you can use the remove urls tool to remove a web page from the SERPs for any reason.

9. **Change of Address Tool**
   Instead of losing all that link juice from an old or aliased domain name, you can issue a change of

address request and get that link juice redirected. Just like mail redirection at the post office, except that it's free and your neighbour doesn't accidentally get your post half the time.

10. **Broken Links tool**

Of course you don't have any broken links, this tool is for other people who don't regularly check links like you do meticulously every day.

11. **Page Speed Insights**

Does exactly what it says on the tin – lets you know which pages load slowly and gives suggestions how to fix them. It has been recently updated to show mobile and desktop versions separately. Even better, it automatically creates optimised versions of your images, JavaScript and CSS resources saving you time and effort doing this. Just download the optimised versions and upload to your site.

There are lots of other tools for specialised tasks, and Google frequently add and change the tools available. It's worth checking GWT at least every few weeks. It's free and very handy so there's no reason not to.

4.7 Disavow Bad Links

Before the Penguin came (the update I mean, not batman's enemy), Google ignored spammy and low quality links when calculating your page rankings. After the update, it included this data when calculating your site's quality. Spammers, Hackers and Black Hat SEOers rejoiced as this meant that negative SEO was much easier (see chapter 7 for more info on negative SEO).

Effectively, to downgrade a competitor's website, all you needed to do was create automated spammy links back to their site. Similar to the old way of generating higher rankings from automated links, the same methods were then employed. This is one example of where white hat SEO turns Black Hat. In response to this danger, Google created a tool to 'disavow' such spammy back links. Once a site owner disavows a spammy link, Google then treats that backlink as if it didn't exist.

To disavow links you have to log into your Google webmaster tools account (you do have one don't you?) and then follow this procedure:

1. Click on the affected site.
2. Click 'search traffic' on the dashboard
3. Click 'links to your site'
4. Under 'who links the most' click 'more'
5. Click 'download more sample links' or 'download latest links' if the spam links are recent.
6. Copy the spam links from this file into a .txt file
7. If you want to exclude a whole domain insert 'domain:www.spammydomain.com'

8. Go to the 'disavow links tool page' (https://www.Google.com/webmasters/tools/disavow-links-main)
9. Select your website from the drop down
10. Click 'disavow links' and select your txt file to upload

It should take a few days to Google to process the file, and in some cases can take several weeks for large numbers of links.

4.8 Responsive Design

Tuesday April 21st 2015

This date marked the start of what some doomsayers called "Mobigeddon". On this day, Google released a major update to its mobile search algorithm which downgraded sites that were not mobile compatible, and boosted the rankings of websites that were mobile friendly.

Predictions of massive crashes in search traffic were generally over exaggerated (and generally spread by the spam emails of web design companies trying to sell mobile websites) but there was a general agreement that the impact on search traffic was noticeable and significant.

Between 40% and 60% of search traffic are said to come from mobile devices - figures vary depending on which source you consult, but the trend is definitely going in the direction of more mobile sessions and fewer desktop sessions.
So how do you make a website mobile friendly? There are 3 options:

1. Create a simple website with large text that flows across the screen
2. Create a separate website for mobile versions and use browser detection to redirect people
3. Create a website that is fluid in design and responds to the width of the browser window gracefully.

Option 2 was the most popular method up until 2013. Until this time, browser support for the more advanced features of CSS was not strong enough to allow websites to get away with it.

These days, nearly all browsers support CSS media queries which are the cornerstone of making a website responsive.

CSS Media Queries

What's a CSS Media Query I hear you say? Well, in a nutshell, a media query if a special form of style sheet rule that allows you to specify the maximum and minimum browser size which the rules should operate in. Consider the following example:

```
<div id="leftdiv">this is on the left</div>
<div id="rightdiv">This is on the right</div>

<style>
#leftdiv{float:left;width:350px}
#rightdiv{float:left;width:350px}
</style>
```

This would produce a page that has the two lines of text next to each other like this:

```
this is on the left      This is on the right
```

If you viewed the page on a narrow screen, you could have text overlapping the edge of the screen. In some cases you can fix this by using width:50% instead of fixed width size, but if you have a table or image in one of the columns, this can cause problems.

What you can do in this case is to add extra rules in to make the page layout change depending on the size of the browser window. For example:

```
<div id="leftdiv">this is on the left</div>
<div id="rightdiv">This is on the right</div>

<style>
    #leftdiv{float:none;width:100%}
    #rightdiv{float:none;width:100%}
    @media only screen and (min-width: 700px)
    {
        #leftdiv{float:left;width:350px}
        #rightdiv{float:left;width:350px}
    }
</style>
```

So if you view this page in a browser wider than 700px you will see two columns of content, but resize the browser down below 700px wide and you will see one column of content. Note that we put the mobile styles first then use "min-width: 700px" afterwards to cater for wider screen sizes. This method is called 'mobile first' responsive strategy. You could do it the other way round and make the stylesheets "desktop first".

The argument for using mobile first strategy is that it creates more streamlined code for mobile versions, and then the more complex css is handled by desktops. The advantage of doing desktop first is that you don't need to add any hacks to make it work in IE8 (although few people use IE8 now anyway). It is generally considered good practice now to use 'mobile first' responsive layouts.

What widths should you design for?

It's not really worth looking at the screen sizes of different devices when considering where to make your media size boundaries. The reason for this is that there are so many different device browser sizes, and even if you target the latest iPhone size, there's no telling when an ultra HD display device might come along and change things. Therefore you should set your design widths according to how your individual design looks. Make sure you consider all pages on your site too. Some pages might have large tables of data which are difficult to resize down, or they may have detailed images which need to be viewed in the largest possible size.

Summary

These days, all websites should be mobile friendly (with a few exceptions for complex admin systems that are not appropriate for mobile delivery). The best way to achieve mobile friendly websites it to use mobile first responsive web design.

4.9 Local and Personalised Search

Let's say you have a business. Let's make it a painting and decorating business. You have a van. It's not a very good van, but it gets you around. You generally work in your local area, but once in a while you might have to go out of town for the odd job. You want to get more business so you ask a chap you know to make you a website and get some business from that. After the websites been up for a couple of weeks you get an email from a lady in New Hampshire wanting a quote for painting her kitchen. Problem is, you live in Huddersfield so this lead is completely useless to you. So what is the point of trying to get to the top of search engines for 'painting and decorating services' when over 99% of the internet population live outside your area?

Businesses that deliver local services are wasting time and money if they are advertising to the wrong crowd. You can spend a year on SEO but if the leads you get are not converting into real jobs, then it's not worth it.

In this case, you should be focussing your online marketing at local search. Google is very good when it comes to pinning down websites to real world locations. It uses data from both Google maps and Google business to show searchers the most relevant local results at the top of any local search. By 'local search', I mean any web search that includes a location in the name, for example, 'hospitals in Manchester' or 'car repair London'. Usually local searches produce a map with marker points on it at the top of the SERPs.

How do I get listed in local search?

The first step to getting listed is to set up a Google My Business account (previously called Google Places). This is a free service. Just go to https://www.Google.com/business/befound.html and once logged in, you will be presented with a tour of the features and instructions on how to set it up. It's pretty easy to set up really, all you need to do is enter your business name, phone numbers, street address, business category and website url. After that your need to verify your business listing. Generally this can be done with either a pin number sent via SMS, or you can get Google to send you a postcard with the pin number on it (both these verification methods are also free to use).

Recently Google My Business has been upgraded so you can now update your Google+, Insights, Reviews and access Google Analytics from the same dashboard. If all this sounds a bit overwhelming, then don't worry, you don't need to use all these features just to get a local Google listing, but at some point in the future, after you have got your listing, you can explore and experiment with these features if you think they might be useful. There is now a mobile app to access Google My Business so you can use these tools anywhere.

Another key way to get listed in local search is to have your company address in the footer of your website. Including the postcode is important here as the automated Google map system finds it easier to index addresses with postcodes.

For some industries, there are local business directories that you can get listed in, some examples are ratedpeople.com, and yahoo small business (which charges $30 per month for inclusion).

Another way to get listed in local search is to get reviews on sites like yelp.com and foursquare. Generally, sites with higher reviews get higher rankings in the Google Local Pack These are the dozen or so sites with map markers that appear at the top of the results, although it appears that google have just reduced the number of sites in the local pack in the last week, for reasons as yet unknown.

If your website has a locations or contact page, including an embedded Google map of your location is a good signal for Google to include your site in location search results. Finally, you can add relevant location information in your site's content. Street names, names of local areas, local landmarks (pubs are great for this for some reason) and local events all help. Some websites create local specific content in sub-pages to specifically target local areas. This works quite well at the minute, but I think the practice is a grey hat area, so best avoided really in case an algorithm update wipes you off the map.

Personalised Search Results

Personalised search is what happens when Google modifies your search results based on what it knows about you. If you have a Google account and are signed in, then Google will have a lot of information about what sites you have visited previously, where you are, where you have been, and what sorts of things interest you. There are 3 main aspects to personalised search:

1. **Search History.**

   When you click on a website link in Googles SERPs (or indeed, when you use Google image search, Google maps, news, shopping, books or just about any other Google search tool) this information is stored in your Google account profile and is used to influence future search results. For example, if you have previously clicked on a lot of pages about cars, then a search for 'oil' will more likely bring up car related websites, but if you have previously clicked on links to pages about the environmental impact of onshore fracking, then the same search will be more likely to give you pages related to the oil and gas industry. If you use Googles search but are not signed in to a Google account, then search history is not recorded. You can tell Google to clear your history, or tell it not to record your web and app activity, but few people know about or use this option.

2. **Bounce Rate.**

   Google can calculate how much time you spend on a website by measuring how long between clicking on links in the search results. If you only spend a short amount of time on a site before trying another link, then that is a signal to Google that the page you visited is of no interest to you, and should therefore be ranked lower in subsequent searches.

3. **Country.**

   Your country and location will change the sort of sites you see. Country-based search has been around for a long time. If you are in the uk and type in 'Google.com' in your browser's address bar, most likely you will be redirected to 'Google.co.uk'. This has more emphasis on UK websites but also includes international sites.

4. **GEO Location**.
   If type into Google 'garages near me', the search engine will use your geo location to generate the results. Mobile search routinely uses geo location services to modify search results, although you can turn off location services in your mobile device.

5. **Platform**.
   If you are using Google on a mobile phone, the chances are you will see different results from searches made on a desktop. If a site is not deemed 'mobile friendly' then it will be downgraded on mobile search.

6. **Time of Day/date of year**.
   There is some evidence that the time of day and the date of the year influences search results. Around Christmas, the search results are more likely to show seasonal results.

7. **Social Connections**.
   One of the newer ranking factors is social media. If a friend in Google+ has reviewed a restaurant, or a game, or shared an article on a particular subject, then related searches are more likely to bring up these results. At present Google use Google+ for social ranking factors, whereas Bing uses Twitter. This situation is likely to change once Google+ is phased out completely so another social ranking factor may be used in the future.

Do you need to be signed in to Google to see personalised search?

In the previous page, I said "If you use Googles search but are not signed in to a Google account, then search history is not recorded" This is not the same as saying you need to be signed in to Google to see personalised search results. Google will modify your search results on any or all of the other factors.

Summary

Personalised search is becoming more common. More people are using Google when signed in to their Google account, so getting traffic when personalised search is turned on is more difficult. However there are ways to use personalised search to your advantage, here are a few:

1. Create multiple locations and localised content. This might involve making multilingual versions of your website, or even having a UK/US version of your site. If you have a business that operates in multiple areas, such as a franchise or hospital group, then create a separate page for each location and optimise the local content. Make sure the local phone number and address are on this page.

2. Encourage people to write reviews on your content so they appear in their social connections and their

friend's social connections.

3. Consider PPC (pay per click) – even if people click on your ad, but don't go through to conversion or purchase, this will still log the page in their history so future searches will make your page rank higher.

4. Make sure pages are accessible on all platforms. This is something that you should be doing anyway, but recent changes in mobile search, and the increasing proportion of non-desktop browsing makes it important that you use responsive mobile friendly websites.

5. Focus on top results. Most searchers will click on the first 3 results in any search. Therefore, if you are not in the top 3, then you won't get included in their search history, and once there, personalised search will make these results higher for that person. Therefore it is better to have a fewer number of keywords have top 3 rankings, than having lots of keywords with the bottom half of page 1 rankings.

6. Make your content engaging and make your page titles and descriptions accurate to the page to increase the amount of time people spend on your page. This will reduce the bounce rate and therefore signal to Google that the page is useful to the searcher.

4.10 SEO for YouTube

Have you noticed that YouTube videos quite often appear at the top of search results in Google? Not surprising really since Google own YouTube.

Search for the name 'Myke Black' and just under the first 2 or 3 results, you'll get a video from a Scottish singer songwriter of the same name. Now wouldn't that be useful to get a video link right at the top of Google for your keywords? Well the good news is that it's not that hard to get there. Consider the number of pages in Googles search index compared to the number of videos in YouTube. An order of thousands or possibly millions fewer. Therefore, for any given keyword you are much more likely to get top rankings in YouTube than you are in Google's natural search, and because YouTube videos also appear in search, you will have a top ranked place in both YouTube search and Google search with much less effort. Google's search engine uses many complex factors for determining page rankings. However, the YouTube system is less complex and uses fewer ranking factors. It seems that YouTube focus more on on-page factors to determine rankings.

Let's consider an example, say you want to rank highly for the phrase 'children's mountain bikes' as quick search in google gives me 2.4 million results (the number is likely to be different if you try it because of personalised search and location factors). In YouTube, the same search gives me 100k results. A much easier target. If you want to be more specific, you can use 'children's mountain bikes for sale' – 2.8 million results in Google, 7k results in YouTube. Now we're getting somewhere. If I just wanted to create an advert for 'children's mountain bikes for sale' I could make it as a video, post on YouTube, and optimise it to get top there, then when someone does a search in google, they will get my video.

To get higher rankings in YouTube, you can do the following:

1. Make sure your video title contains the keyphrase you are interested in, but try not to appear spammy. Best to put the phrase at the start of the video title and keep the title short.
2. Use the phrase in your video description, again avoid spammy text and make it descriptive and enticing.
3. Have the keyword in your video filename.
4. Add tags for your submission and make sure the keyword is the first tag you add. Subsequent tags should be semantically related to your keyword
5. Embed the video in a page on your website which is also optimised for the keyword. Here it is a good idea to include lots of relevant keyword rich content (see chapter 3.7 Creating Great Quality Content).
6. Use speech in the video with the keyword in and then edit the caption transcription for the video so the keywords are identified correctly in the auto captions.

7. Monitor the comments under the video. Remove spam ones and reply to comments to engage audiences and encourage more comments. Each comment will search as a social signal for YouTube.

This is only half of the story though. After they view the video, you want to capture that view and pass it on to your website.

Firstly, you should associate your YouTube account with a website. To do this, you need to verify the website in your Google Webmaster Tools account, and then verify your YouTube channel by going to go to www.youtube.com/verify. After this, go to the advanced channel settings and enter your website under "associated website"

Fig 14: Adding an associated website in Google Webmaster Tools

This will then create backlinks to your website from your YouTube channel.

You can also create backlinks by creating YouTube channel profile links. Go to the Channel page and click on the 'About' tab. Then go to the 'custom links' fields to add as many links as you like, including internal page links, but make sure that the main page link is the first one.

For creating backlinks from individual videos you can add links in video descriptions and comments, and you can also add links within the videos themselves by using annotations to create link overlays on parts of the video. Note though that annotations don't work on mobile devices.

So there we have it- high ranking results in google with backlinks to your website is relatively simple using YouTube SEO.

Chapter 5. Measuring Success

5.1 Visits, users, sessions and hits

How do you know whether your online marketing is working? Maybe your sales increase, or maybe your phones get busier, but that does not mean it's the SEO at work. Perhaps you have real world advertising running in tandem (and if you don't, then you should be).

Measuring the effectiveness of your SEO is vital in knowing what is and what is not working for you. The most obvious way of measuring your SEO effectiveness is by looking at how much your website is being used – something called "website traffic" in the biz. There are a number of ways of measuring traffic – the most frequently used are hits, sessions, visits and users.

So what's the different between a visit, user, session and hit? Let me put it this way. Imagine you go to a friend's house. You enter the front door, switch on the light, go to the kitchen, open the fridge, take a can of beer, drink it, put the empty can in the bin, close the fridge door, leave the kitchen, turn off light, leave the house, then close the front door. Then you go back 10 minutes later, do the same thing again, drinking a second can of beer before leaving. After about an hour, you get thirsty again and decide to raid his fridge a third time.

Thais whole sequence of events is performed by a single 'user' because there is only one visitor at the house during the day. If I came back the next day and stole some more beer it would count as a returning user.

Each action you take (turning on lights, drinking beer etc.) is a 'hit'. In websites, a hit is when any file is requested from the server, so a single webpage with 10 images on it would count as 11 hits.

Each set of visits counts as a 'session'. Most websites measure a session as a set of actions that take place within an average browsing session. A browsing session is deemed to have ended when there is around 20-30 minutes of no activity. So in the beer raid above, there would be 2 sessions since there was an hour between the second and third visit. Google uses 30 minutes to describe a session, whereas different websites might use different lengths of time. Banking websites typically use short session times - which is why if you log in to your online bank account and don't do anything for 15 minutes you will get a 'session timed out' message. The shorter a session is, the more secure the website is (reduced chance that someone might sneak on to your computer when you left it logged in), but also the more annoying for users if they have to re-enter passwords.

The word 'visit' is often used interchangeably with 'session'. While some marketeers have recommended for a slightly different definition for each, according to google analytics they are one and the same, so most people just use this as a convention rather than a standard.

The question of whether to measure your website's traffic in terms of hits, sessions, users or visits will depend partly on what data you need to show. In the old days, when web pages had few embedded files, hits were generally used (and often you would hear phrases like "I get 10,000 hits to my site a month"). Hits are a very bad way to measure traffic. You will probably have no idea how much beer you lost if you try to measure it in terms of single actions. You should measure users or sessions, which are a more accurate measure of how often your fridge is raided, and how much beer you will lose.

Whichever measure you decide to use, you are going to need tools to measure it, and this is where Google Analytics will become your best friend. (Let's just hope it's not the house-breaking-beer-stealing kind of friend though).

5.2 Introduction to Google Analytics

Website traffic monitoring software comes in 2 flavours. There's one kind that sits on your server and analyses log files, then there's the other kind that requires you to add some JavaScript to your web pages and logs each time the script is initiated. Server based traffic software tends to be more accurate, but is also far more expensive. If you want cheap and good quality traffic monitoring tools, then Google Analytics (GA) is the best free option.

At first glance, Google Analytics is daunting. It has grown more powerful over the years but at the same time, more complex. About 90% of the options in GA are quite advanced and not really used very often for simple traffic monitoring. To start using GA, you will need a google account, which is free to get. Once you have an account, go to https://www.google.com/analytics and click on the button at the top labelled 'access google analytics'.

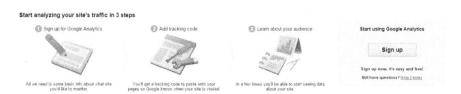

Fig 15: Initial setup process for Google Analytics

Click on the signup button and then enter some details:

Account name – this is the name that you will use for your google analytics account, and all websites are stored in these 'accounts'. Note you should only have one google account, but you can create multiple analytics accounts. This is useful if you are an SEO company and need to track groups of websites separately from each other. Currently the limit is 100 analytics accounts, but if you need to create more than 100 you will need to register a second google account.

Website name - The name of your website is not so important. Generally we use the website address as the name since sometimes websites change their names but have the same address.

Website URL – put here the primary url for the website. If your website uses more than one address, e.g. .co.uk and .com versions, then it is better to put the one that appears on your business cards and stationary. Note if you use redirects on your website, then put the URL of the target site.

Industry Category – select the most relevant. This option is not really used much so not important if you don't find an applicable category here.

After you have entered this information, click on the 'get tracking id' button, then accept the terms of service in the popup.

The next page will show you your tracking code. It will probably look something like this:

```
<script>
(function(i,s,o,g,r,a,m){i['GoogleAnalyticsObject'
]=r;i[r]=i[r]||function(){

(i[r].q=i[r].q||[]).push(arguments)},i[r].l=1*new
Date();
a=s.createElement(o),m=s.getElementsByTagName(o)[0
]; a.async=1; a.src=g;
m.parentNode.insertBefore(a,m)
  })(window,document,'script','//www.google-
analytics.com/analytics.js','ga');
  ga('create', 'UA-XXXXXXXX-1', 'auto');
  ga('send', 'pageview');
</script>
```

You will need to copy this code into every page of your website.

Once the code is in your site, you can start tracking your visitors. Click on 'home' at the top, then on 'All Web Site Data'. To test your code is working, select 'Real-Time' > 'Overview' in the left hand panel then open your website in a new browser window. You will see, if the code is working correctly, the activity will be shown in the real time monitor and you will be able to see information about who is on your site right now, where they came from, where they live, and what pages they are looking at.

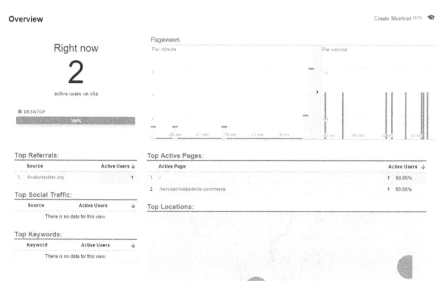

Fig 16: Google Analytics real time statistics view

To view your website traffic, you will need to click on 'Audience' > 'Overview'. This will give you a snapshot of your traffic in the time period selected. (To change the time period, click on the dates in the top right corner).

The most useful traffic measurements in Google Analytics are:

1. Number of users/sessions - this will show you how many people have visited your site in a certain time period. Generally on established sites we like to

compare traffic on a year by year basis. This is because there are seasonal variations in traffic that are affected by things like summer holidays or Christmas periods and there are regular patterns of activity over the year. Comparing traffic on a month by month basis is generally not a good indicator of performance (even though Google Analytics uses monthly comparisons in traffic trends).

2. % of new visits - knowing how many potentially new customers are visiting your site will give you a good understanding on how your marketing is going. If a large proportion of your site is new customers then that is a sign that you are reaching new audiences, but if your business model relies on repeat custom then having few returning visitors is not a good sign.

3. Pages per visit – a low number of pages per visit means your site is not engaging, and people are unwilling to find out more about you. The exception to this is the one-page website templates that are becoming more popular.

4. Page views – the number of pages that were viewed in total, the higher the better.

Other useful information includes:

1. Landing and Exit pages (Behaviour > Site Content > Landing Pages) - entry and exit points for your website will let you know what people are looking for (landing

pages) and when they leave it means they have either found what they wanted, e.g. payment confirmation on ecom site, or they have given up. Examining your exit pages is a good way of enhancing your site's experience.

2. Referral sources (Acquisition > All Traffic > Referrals) – knowing where traffic comes from is vital in online marketing as it lets you know what is it that you did which generated the best results. Until a couple of years ago, you could get good information on what keywords people used in google to find your site. Nowadays more searchers use https version of google which means that referral keywords cannot be passed through to your website, so the referral keyword is just listed as 'not provided'. This is a great loss in SEO, although you can get some info about referring keywords from google webmaster tools, but it will not allow you to examine which referrals generate the best quality of traffic.

You can use the search bar at the top of the left hand side to find other reports quickly if you are not sure where to find them in the menu.

5.3 Advanced Google Analytics Techniques

Now that you have the full power of Google Analytics behind your site, you can start using it to find out interesting information. You can find out things like who is visiting your website, what pages they looked at, what information they are looking for, and why they left. You can use ecom tracking to find out which products are more popular in different countries, or you can find out what search queries people use in your site. This and a thousand other questions can be answered with the data gathered by google analytics, but mining this information can be a complex task.

Here are a few examples of the advanced tools in Google Analytics:

1. **Event tracking**.

   Event tracking means logging individual actions, like when a button is clicked, or a video is played, or anything that can generate a JavaScript call (including Ajax requests that don't initiate a page load). To use this, you need to attach extra tracking code to your web page to catch these events and pass that information on to the GA. With event tracking you can determine a lot of information.

2. **Ecommerce tracking**.

   Ecom tracking is very handy. It can register when products are bought, their value, product category, billing locations, and campaigns. So for example, if you set up a pay per click campaign in google AdWords, you can track the value of sales that came from this campaign. You can also segregate the data, so you can tell things like how many sales were made on mobile devices, how much was sold in different countries, or which product categories had the best conversion rates. This is a great tool if you want to use A-B testing to try out different layouts of product pages to see whether conversion rates would change with a new layout.

3. **Goals and Funnels**

   Goals are a way of measuring whether your site fulfils its target objectives. Quite often, it is used on contact pages of websites where the primary aim of the website is to attract more business, or on download pages where the aim of the site is to get people to download something. 'Funnels' are the routes through to that objective. So for example, if you have a website with 3 pages to your purchase page, you can create a funnel to see how many people drop out from the site in each page (typically this will look like a funnel shape). In the illustration below, you can see how many people drop out of the buying process at each stage.

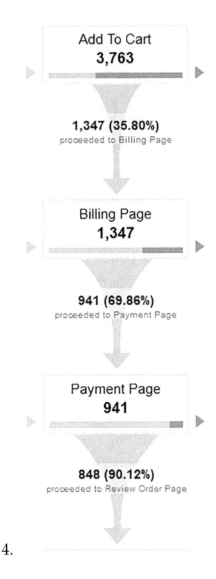

4.

Fig 17: Dropout rates in goal funnels

5. **Campaign Tracking**

   Google Analytics integrates with Google AdWords to
   give you information on who is clicking on your ads,
   and what they do after they have clicked on your ad.

This can give you great feedback on the quality of the ad's landing pages, and the routes people use to get to the goals. You can also add tracking code to links in marketing emails and banner ads to track this activity in your analytics.

6. **Site Search**

   If your site has a search facility, you can track the phrases that people use in your search bar. If your users are looking for a certain topic, you can tell which pages they visit on your site after searching. It is a very useful way of finding out what you need to add on your website to engage customer interest.

7. **Filters**

   If you want to exclude data from visitors within your own organisation, or from other irrelevant sources, then you can add filters. If you are beset by analytics spam (see 5.4 below) then you can filter out this traffic from your reports. Another use for filters is to exclude data from particular regions or from specific ad campaigns.

8. **Demographics and Interests**

   Analytics allows you to view demographic information on your visitors. This information comes from third parties like doubleclick.com, android advertising ID and iOS Identifier for Advertisers (IDFA). This data will only come from a portion of your visitors so should be regarded as sampling data, rather than actual data. If there are not enough people in the demographics, the data is not shown and you will see a message saying "some data in this report may have been removed when a threshold was applied". This is to prevent details of individual users being identified from the information. In some cases you might like to know this information for remarketing opportunities, which is where Visitor Intelligence is required (see 5.6 below).

9. **Schedule Email Reports.**

One of the best features of Google Analytics is that you can set up reports to send on a schedule basis to your email. This automation saves a lot of time recreating reports, and is especially useful for online marketing companies which have to monitor the traffic of a large number of websites. To set up a scheduled email, you need to first create a report (which is basically any view in analytics) then click on 'email' at the top. You can add more reports to the email after you have first created it. Emails are sent for 12 months only so after that time you will have to reschedule the email to send again.

To add a report to this email, load up the report in analytics, then click on email and then in the bottom right corner of the popup click on 'add to existing email'

To view and edit reports you need to go to the 'View Assets' option. To do this, go to 'admin' at the top, then in the 3rd column under 'view' go down to 'scheduled emails'. On this page you will see a list of scheduled emails. Click on the subject name to edit the email, or to extend or delete the email, click on the actions drop down at the right of the table. You can select to extend the schedule for another 12 months or delete it here.

5.4 Shortcomings of Google Analytics

Analytics is an amazing product. To fully explore its features would require a whole book in itself. But it does have a few issues. Three of these are Analytics spam, missing referral keywords, and lack of visitor intelligence.

Analytics spam

Recently analytics spam has become a big problem. Sites like 4webmasters.org, buttons-for-websites.com and other (mainly Russian) spam sites have been using spam bots to create 'ghost visits' on websites. They do this is by reproducing the JavaScript tracking code and using your 'web property id' (the analytics tracking code id for your website) to send a lot of fake referral hits to analytics. Some of the bots that do this do not even visit your website, so you cannot block them with htaccess or firewall filters.

You can prevent this issue to some extent by using Google Tag Manager, but if your analytics ID is already being used then tactic this will not stop the referral spam. Currently, the only way to fix it is by creating another web property id - which will require getting new tracking code and starting with a new data set. If you do this you cannot access previous traffic data from your new analytics account. One you have a new web property id, you should use Google Tag Manager to hide it from bots.

You can block individual sites using a custom advanced filter. Go to Admin and select 'filters'.
Then click on the big red button to create a new filter.

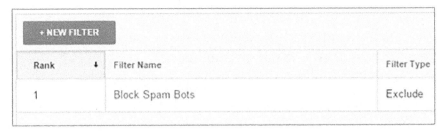

Fig 18: adding a filter in Google Analytics

Give the filter a name, then select 'custom' in the filter type. Select 'exclude' radio button and in the filter field dropdown select 'request URI'. Then in the filter pattern but in the referral URL of the spammy site.

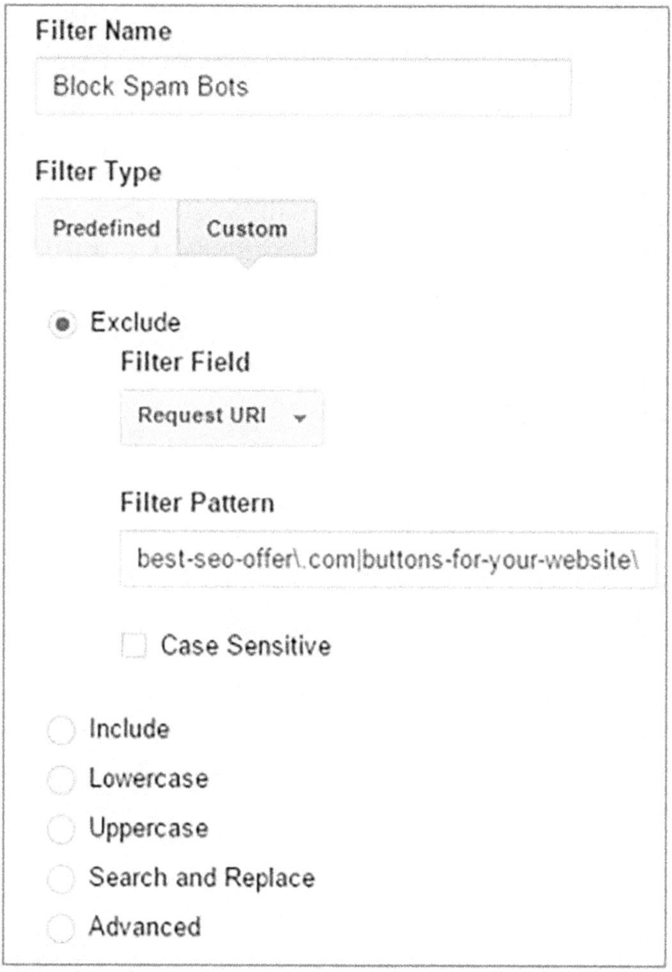

Filter Name

Block Spam Bots

Filter Type

Predefined   Custom

● Exclude

Filter Field

Request URI ▾

Filter Pattern

best-seo-offer\.com|buttons-for-your-website\

☐ Case Sensitive

○ Include

○ Lowercase

○ Uppercase

○ Search and Replace

○ Advanced

Fig 19: Excluding hostnames from Google Analytics using filters

Note, this will not remove any historical data, it will only remove future hits from this spambot.

Using the hostnames filters works well enough, but the problem with analytics spammers is that they often change hostnames when one becomes blocked. A better system is to block the spammers' countries. If you are not too bothered about recording traffic from Russia, Indonesia and Brazil, then it's better to create a filter which will block these countries. This will more or less eliminate all of the spam traffic without having to keep checking what hostnames the spammers are using every week. The procedure for blocking countries is very similar, except in the Filter Field, type in 'Country' and then enter the country in the Filter Pattern field. You will have to create a filter for each country.

Why do analytics spammers do this? Well, quite often the spam site hosts malicious software to infect your browser, or they use online advertising and them spam referrals in the hope that you will click on the site to see what's there, and then they will get lots of hits to their hosted ads and make money from it. Their click through rate in percentage is extremely tiny, but because they spam so many websites, their traffic is significant.

Missing Referral Keywords

Before google started using SSL for web search, you could see what keywords people used in google to find your website. This was incredibly useful for SEO. Now, nearly all referral keywords show up as 'not provided' in GA's referral reports. This is not helpful at all.

If you want to see what kind of keywords people are using to get to your website, then you can use Google Webmaster Tools. But this information is incomplete and not very accurate.

There is however a way of getting some data from the 'not provided' keywords. You can create a view which will convert the 'not provided' links to show you which pages these links go to.

The procedure is this:

1. Create a new view by going to 'admin' then in the drop down under 'view' in the right hand column, select 'create new view' (we should keep the original view as this new view might exclude some data)
2. Give your reporting view a new name like 'Referrals' and select the time zone, then click 'Create view'
3. Then when you get back to the admin screen select 'filters' in the right column.
4. Click on the big red 'create new filter' button
5. Give the filter a name like 'referral filter' and under 'Filter type' select 'custom'.

6. Select the bottom option 'advanced' which will then display a few more fields. Fill in the fields like the screenshot below:

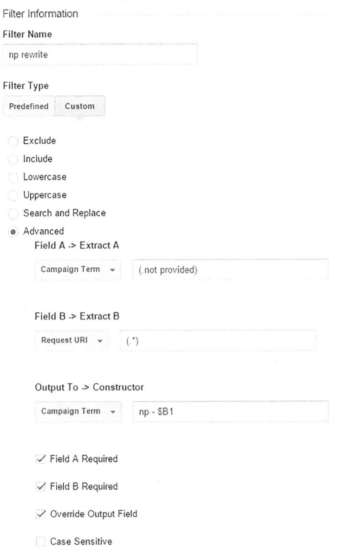

Fig 20: Adding a filter to view 'not provided' data.

Click 'save' to create the filter. Test it out by going to https://google.com (if you get redirected to a non-secure version of google then click on 'use google.com ' in the bottom right). Enter a search term for which you know your site will be listed, then click on the link. In a couple of hours you should see your hit in google analytics. If it has worked, in the referral keywords, you will see something like 'np-[your keyword]' instead of 'not provided'.

Thanks to Dan Barker of econsultancy.com for sharing this method.

Visitor Intelligence in Google Analytics

One major downside to analytics is that it does not give you data about individuals. We know that it holds this data because it can display demographics about age, gender, interests and other useful things, but because of data protection issues, google analytics is not allowed to display data about individuals.

5.5 Visitor Intelligence

Visitor Intelligence means proactively collecting information about a visitor from data capture and behaviour in order to gain new leads and sales opportunities. Each visitor to your website has a value. Some are high value (quite likely to purchase or quite likely to gain a higher ROI) and some are low value (less likely to purchase or have lower ROI). Visitor intelligence is a means of scoring each individual on a scale of value and accessibility. To do this, we would like to know certain things like job title, contact email, company size, and industry type, past purchasing history, age, gender, salary level, home address, interests, and a whole load of things relevant to what you are selling. Google Analytics cannot do this, but there are products that can. They work by offering incentives for sharing personal information, such as a survey in which you could win a prize, or a simple name and email field to download a free pdf document. Once you have these snippets of information you can stitch them together to get a profile of the visitor. Using web tracking and email tracking with user identifiable tracking cookies, you can get a picture of the sorts of pages these people visit, or the sorts of email marketing that they click on and other aspects of their online behaviour.

Once you have a list of visitors along with their intelligence data, you can then convert them into prospects (potential customers) and prioritise them to follow up leads. This could be by phone, text or email. You could even send out invites to conferences and events that you think they might be interested in. For example, if you have a 20 year old woman with a high level of disposable income who is visiting your cosmetic surgery site, you might want to send out a personalised invitation to an open day at the clinic. If it's an 80 year old man looking at the breast enlargement pages on your site, then you probably wouldn't want to send out the invite to them.

There are many products like Canndi (http://www.canddi.com/) and Zoho (https://www.zoho.com/) out there which have great visitor intelligence facilities and will help you generate leads for your business if you know how to harness that data into a meaningful way.
Visitor Intelligence also helps with SEO. It can determine which keywords are most likely to convert into a good lead, and which are not so you can focus on the more important keywords in your online marketing.

Chapter 6. When SEO goes wrong

6.1 How to avoid Google Penalisation.

Sometimes SEO marketeers get things wrong. If you use grey hat tactics, you might find that what was once acceptible, is no longer ok, and you might discover your site that used to rank well seems to fall out of google like a fat man climbing a thin tree. This is how it feels to get penalised by google. Sometimes rankings drop due to changes in the algorithm, and if you have stopped getting traffic, this is the first thing to consider. You have to do a lot to get penalised, and the more established a website it, the harder it is to get banned from the index, but it can and does happen even to large websites.

Google never penalise sites without a good reason. Generally it's because of over aggressive marketing, breaking the webmaster rules, or your site getting hacked.

Over aggressive marketing can occur if your site suddenly starts getting lots of backlinks. Any unnatural link growth can be seen as questionable, especially if the backlinks come from pages on different topics to your own site. You need to keep on top of your backlink monitoring to make sure you are not getting spammed. You can always disavow any links that you think are harmful in google webmaster tools.

Breaking the webmaster guidelines is also a good way to get a penalty, so read these and make sure your site does not break any of them (think of them as the internet equivalent of the 10 commandments).

Your website quality is also a factor. If you add or change content so that google thinks it looks spammy, this may get you penalised. It's unlikely unless you really go to town on your keyword spamming but it can and does happen. So the moral is, make sure your site is consistently good quality content and don't try to risk going too far into the dark side.

6.2 Duplicate content penalty

Copying content from another website is terribly bad form. Google doesn't like it, and I'm sure that the person who wrote the copy won't like it either. Not only does it mean you are lazy and dishonest, but it also means that people reading your content won't be getting the best source of information.

If you steal your content, then at best, your web page will not show up in search engines at all. But if you have a lot of duplicated content on lots of pages on your site, you may find your domain name is shunned entirely. Generally duplicate content is created when automated programs called 'screen scrapers' are used to try to fool google into giving them equally high rankings to those pages that they stole the copy from. This used to work 10 years ago, but now does not. In general, if a site is already in google with the same copy, then the newly found page will not be included in the main index.

Duplicate content might also be mistakenly created on your website, for example, if you have two different urls that serve up the same content, Google might not know which page to include from the two and which is the original. Websites that use www addresses like http://www.mysite.com are seen as different urls from the non www address http://mysite.com. Sometimes you will get pages indexed from both domains but with lower trust rankings. Other mistaken duplications might occur when using dynamic urls to get content. For example mysite.com/index.php?page=2 is a different url to mysite.com/index.php?page=2&section=4.

In order to prevent this, you can add rel=canonical tags in the <head> section of your webpage. Canonical tags look something like this:

```
<link rel="canonical"
href="https://mysite.com/index.php?page=2" />
```

Another way of telling google about mirror urls is to set the preferred domain in Google Webmaster Tools. This is a much better way than using canonical tags because it helps with the link weighting on the page. All links from the non-preferred domain are counted as being from the preferred domain, so the linking power of the page is not diluted.

Incidentally, if you have both http and https versions of your site, it's better to use https as the preferred domain (as long as the SSL certificate is valid) because google gives higher rankings to secure urls.

6.3 Payday loan penalty

In June 2013, Google published an algorithm update that specifically addressed those sites which heavily spammed queries such as 'payday loans', 'viagra', and 'penis enlargement' and some porn related keywords. Since then there have been a few changes to this part of the algorithm.

It is difficult to accidentally get this type of penalty. Typically those sites that are affected are involved in link chain schemes, have very low quality content, and often include illegal activities like phishing scams.

6.4 EMD Penalty

EMD stands for Exact Matching Domain. This is when you have a website who's URL contains the keyword that you are targeting, such as 'buybikesonline.com'. Often this SEO setup also involves having a large number of backlinks to the site with the keyword as the link text.

Having keywords in your URL used to be a very good SEO strategy but now it's seen as spammy by google. Once you have been hit with this penalty it is very hard to fix it without changing your URL altogether and starting again from scratch.

6.5. Manual Penalties

In addition to the automated penalisation, Google also employ a number of people whose job it is to rate the quality of websites. If a site is flagged as suspicious by google, the quality raters manually check the site to see if it looks ok, and if it appears to them as bad, they have the ability to downgrade the site or even kick it out of google altogether. Sometimes, the manual reviewers revisit pages to see if they have cleaned up or removed malware. This happens when you submit a 'reconsideration request' following warnings of malware. According to Matt Cutts, there are 400,000 manual actions initiated every month (many more are automatically penalised by google and panda updates). Of these, only 20,000 webmasters ever submit a reconsideration request- about 5% of the total number of penalised sites.

If you receive a manual penalty, then you are sent a notification by google telling you what the issue is on your page. This notification will appear in your Google Webmaster Tools account or if you do not have an account, you might get a notification to the admin email address of the domain in question.

6.6 How to recover from Google Penalty

If you believe that you have been hit by a penalty, the first thing to do is check your Google Webmaster Account to see if there are any notifications in there. If there are no notifications, this means you have not incurred a manual penalty.

Next you need to check your site for malware, you might have been hacked so using an online website scanner will help you here.

Check your backlinks, and see if there is a sudden increase in number or if there are a lot that seem spammy. Use the 'disavow links' tool in Google Webmaster Tools to remove any bad links.

It's worth doing a bit of research at this point to see if the drop in rankings correspond with an algorithm update. For this you can check the Google Algorithm Change History page here
https://moz.com/google-algorithm-change
If you find anything that might explain the penalisation, you should fix it as soon as possible, then send google a 'reconsideration request' (again, this is something that you can find in your Google Webmaster Tools account). If you have recently rebuild your website or purchased the domain, then a reconsideration request might help you here also.

Even if you don't find anything wrong with your site and backlinks, it is still worth checking and sending a reconsideration request in case something there was affecting your site is now no longer online e.g. temporary backlink spamming.

Chapter 7 - Negative SEO

7.1 What is Negative SEO?

Negative SEO is the reverse of search engine optimisation. The aim of search engine optimisation is to increase a site's visibility in the SERPs. With Negative SEO, the aim of the procedure is to reduce a page's rankings in the search results. This chapter includes information on how negative SEO can be done, and some of the steps you can do to prevent it from happening to you - or at least reduce the impact.

7.2 Why use negative SEO?

There are three main cases where negative SEO is used:

1. **To downgrade your competitor's sites**
   - to improve your own rankings. This is called **SERP bubbling**. Generally it is performed alongside standard SEO. The aim of SERP bubbling is to affect your website's rankings by forcing down the rankings of those competitors immediately above you, so that your site effectively floats to the top of the SERPs like a bubble in a glass of fizzy cola.

2. **To bury bad news about yourself or your company**
   More and more, we are seeing large corporations, high profile figures and celebrities using Negative SEO marketing experts to downgrade the rankings of pages that are detrimental to their image. This process is

called Search Engine Reputation Management (SERM) - also known as **Online Reputation Management.** Figures on how much this industry is worth are not available due to the sensitive nature of the process, however, there is evidence that this process is becoming more common. The number of companies that offer specialist advice and SERM services is increasing.

3. **Targeted Negative SEO (TNS) attack on the website -** this could be done for political, financial or personal reasons. There is evidence that negative SEO is performed by some animal rights groups against animal testing firms. Some would even argue that China's censorship of politically uncomfortable material amounts to Targeted Negative SEO.

7.3 How is negative SEO done?

There are a number of ways you can eliminate a page from the search engine rankings. Some of the methods listed are legitimate and good practice, but others are sneaky, immoral and probably illegal. This information is provided so that you may prevent your site being a victim of negative SEO, rather than to condone the practice.

1. **Remove the offending content**
    this is the easiest method. If a derogatory post has been made on a forum, you can request that the moderators remove the content. Quite often a polite email is all that is needed. Sometimes a solicitor's letter might help with your argument, but in general, forum moderators and blog owners are quite happy to remove potentially damaging posts and comments.

2. **Promote non offending content - "Insulation"**
    This involves creating or promoting pages that are not harmful, for example, if a page contains negative messages about your client, you can create positive message content, and do SEO to promote those pages higher up, and force the bad press down the rankings where it will have less impact.

    Similarly, you can do this for business competitors. If you sell product A and your competitor sells products A and B, then you can promote another company that just sells product B, which is not in competition with you, but is in competition with the business that you are doing negative SEO on.

This method is sometimes called **Google Insulation.**

3. **Google Bowling**
   This is a technique designed to remove a site from the SERPs by making Google believe the site is spammy. The are two ways this can be done. One is to add links to the site from lots of bad neighbourhoods, link farms and automatically generated spammy pages. If you get thousands of links back to the site in a few days and get them to show up in Google's results, this can trigger a spam alert and affect the rankings of the site. The other way it is done is to find a page on your competitors website which has dynamic URLs but has the same content, for example, if they have a page with the url http://mycompetitor.com/index.php?page=11, then is the url is changed to http://mycompetitor.com/index.php?page=11&rnd=1 but has the same content, then you are vulnerable to Google bowling by url manipulation. What is done then is to create hundreds of links with slightly different urls but the same content, post these links liberally around forums, blogs, directories and link farms, and sooner or later Google will tag it as black hat.

4. **Infect their site**
   If a site is infected with a virus, then it is flagged up in the SERPs as being potentially dangerous. This can be also achieved by using cross site scripting (XSS) vulnerabilities to create links to pages which display on page content from posted form elements or querystrings - for example, if you have a site with a page like search.asp?keyword=mysearch and in the page itself it says 'there are no results for mysearch' - then the link can be manipulated to search.asp?keyword=X where X is a chunk of

pernicious javascript. If you then post this link on another webpage, then anyone clicking on it will get the search results page, and where it says 'there are no results for X' the JavaScript is inserted into the page content and runs with the same security level as the main page itself. When Google picks this link up, it will flag your site as infected and probably remove it from the search results. You might also get a 'this site contains malware' message when you try to visit the link.

5. **Tattling**
   This involved informing Google that a site contravenes its guidelines. Usually this is to report paid-for links (which you yourself could theoretically set up without the target site's involvement), or grey hat SEO tactics used on the site. Other forms of tattling is to claim copyright theft of content or images.

6. **Guilty by Association**
   This method involves making your own spammy site - the spammier the better - using a similar URL to your competitor and if possible use the same domain registrar and hosting services. Copying the metatags and site content of the home page of your target site is also useful. Then you do everything in your power to get the site banned (it's not hard). Once you have done this, you install a 301 redirect to your competitor's site and sit back and watch it slide down the rankings like a pig on a greasy pole! This is especially effective if your shadow site has the same pages as the target site and you do individual 301 redirects to the target site.

7. **False duplicated content**
   The way this is done is to create a site with the same content as your competitor, but try to get the new

content to the site crawled before your competitor. For example, if your competitor changes their home page, you change your duplicate site's homepage to the same content and metatags, then submit a sitemap with just that page on it to Google, Bing and yahoo site explorer, so that your content is indexed first and your competitor's content is ignored as duplicate content when the search engines get around to indexing them. This is very hard to defend against, and only reporting the site as phishing content can save you here. Canonical urls can also help, but not much.

8. **Denial of Service Attacks (DOS)**
   This method of hacking uses several different computers to simultaneously flood the target website with requests so that the volume of traffic blocks up the website's bandwidth and essentially cuts off access to the rest of the world. Distributed denial of service attacks (DDOS) are even more damaging because they use hundreds or even thousands of virus infected zombie PCs all on different IP Addresses to attack the target site.

   If a site is unreachable when Google tries to crawl it, this has negative consequences for the rankings of the site. Recent DDOS attacks on Visa, MasterCard and PayPal in retaliation for their withdrawn support of WikiLeaks are more likely to have an immediate impact, but the reduction in SERPs will have a longer term impact that is impossible to measure

9. **Click Fraud**
   If your competitor has AdWords running for their site, you can click on their adverts to use up their budget and affect the number of genuine visitors. Generally

Google is pretty good at detecting this, so it has limited impact. However, if you set up a team of people in different locations and get them all to do 3 or 4 clicks a day, it soon adds up.

Another click mechanism is to get all your friends to click on your site, or the sites just below your competitor. There is some evidence to suggest that the number of clicks in the search results affects your rankings.

10. **AdSense Banning**

If your target site uses Google AdSense, then you can click on their adverts on their site many times until the AdSense account is suspended. It's much easier to suspend someone's AdSense account than it is to get it resumed following allegations of click fraud.

11. **Black social bookmarking**

This method uses social networking sites like twitter and Facebook to create lots of bogus accounts, then use these accounts to create spammy links to the target site with phrases like 'viagra', 'porn', 'teens', 'warez', 'crackz', 'gambling' etc. This is an extension of Google bowling taking advantage of the new features of Google that include real time search of social networking sites. In recent times, with Google including more Facebook and twitter pages in the SERPs, this technique has become more effective.

12. **Fake Bouncing**

This is another SEO technique that I invented. The way it works is this: it's understood that your site's bounce rate has an effect on Google rankings. The way Google measures this is if you click on a site, then click the back button to get back to the SERPs. The theory is that if people don't spend a lot of time on a page, then it must be low quality. Therefore if you click on your

competitor's pages and click back to the SERPs multiple times over many days, these pages will have a higher reported bounce rate. It works better if you have more than one IP address to do this with. Over time, the increased bounce rates for your competitors will have a negative effect on the site's rankings.

7.4 SEO Piracy

There is a disturbing trend in recent years for SEO piracy. This is when you receive an email out of the blue saying 'pay us $10,000 or we will get your site banned from the search engines'. These **SEO Pirates** generally target vulnerable organisations or businesses, those with good search engine rankings or those using lots of AdWords in the hope of frightening people into paying up. Holding websites to ransom is nothing new, online pirates have demanded ransoms following DOS attacks on LiveJournal and Twitter in 2006, so the SEO piracy is just a new extension on that. Generally though, if you receive an email out of the blue demanding money, you should just bin it and forget about it. It's not normally worth their time pursuing a negative SEO campaign on a target that is unlikely to be able to pay up, and negative SEO does involve a lot of effort and time, which the pirates probably wouldn't want to waste when they can just send the same email out to 1 million businesses and get a return for zero effort.

7.5 How to defend yourself against Negative SEO

To defend against negative SEO, you should monitor your rankings, traffic and backlinks. Normally, if you are hit by negative SEO, you soon find out, as your traffic drops like a stone.

Here are a few tips on how to defend yourself against negative SEO:

1. Make sure you check Bing webmaster tools and Google webmaster tools regularly - also make sure that your email address is set up correctly so you can react to notification emails promptly.

2. If you are hit by a virus or malware, get your website back online as soon as possible, the longer you leave it, the worse it will be.

3. Remove any potentially damaging material from your website and social media. Fix any pages that might have bad links on them, e.g. in Facebook comments from bogus accounts.

4. If it's a DDOS attack, inform your ISP or webhost as they can usually do something to mitigate the damage.

5. Disavow bad backlinks - Bing webmaster tools and Google webmaster tools allow you to report any backlinks from spammy sources.

6. Use reconsideration requests if you have been penalised. These take a little while to get dealt with but

is much faster than just letting Google figure it out on its own.

7. Try to identify the source - sometimes offence is the best defence and if you can prove that a competitor is damaging your websites revenue, you may have grounds to sue.

7.6 Should I use Negative SEO?

At the end of the day, the effort required to damage other people's rankings can better be applied to promoting your own sites. You should only ever use negative SEO give the following conditions:

1. You must have permission of the site owner, or of the person/business about whom the page it directed.

2. You must not contravene any of Google's guidelines.

3. You must not pay for the services of black hat SEO specialists.

4. You must not do anything to damage the website or the servers on which the website is hosted, or install malware or viruses on client machines.

5. You must not create links solely for the purpose or denigrating the reputation of the offending website.

Some people claim that negative SEO does not work because Google would not let that happen. If you don't believe that try googling 'negative SEO' and see who comes out in the top pages. They did not get there by accident.

Section 3 – Off-site marketing

This section focuses on the sorts of marketing that take place outside of your website. This can be on social media, email marketing or even offline marketing.

The section also includes information on how to use online advertising to drive more traffic to your website.

Chapter 8 – Internet Marketing v Marketing Everywhere

8.1 Meet my little friend

We'll start of this chapter with a couple of introductions. I've already introduced ourselves in chapter 1 (if you haven't read that yet, skip back a few pages, it's a corker), but in this chapter I'm going to introduce a couple of friends: IM and ME IM – Internet marketing – is defined as:

Internet marketing, or online marketing, refers to advertising and marketing efforts that use the Web and email to drive direct sales via electronic commerce, in addition to sales leads from Web sites or emails. Internet marketing can also be broken down into more specialized areas such as Web marketing, email marketing and social media marketing:

Source: Webopedia.com

My other friend is ME - Marketing Everywhere - which I define as:

The attempt to make marketing messages ubiquitous, involving internet, mobile messaging, offline media, product sponsorship, social media, and any other medium by which a message can be communicated, either consciously or subconsciously

Source: me, today.

IM is relatively easy to define. ME is more of a nebulous concept. It's the can of Pepsi drank by Marty McFly in Back to the Future; it's is the free pen put into the charity letters; it's the catchy jingle on the radio; it's the window sticker in the car in front of you at the traffic lights. Quite simply put, Marketing Everywhere is marketing that you can see, hear, (or even smell) everywhere you go.

8.2 Compare the marketing (.com)

Some marketing experts believe that ME is the best way to get the largest number of hits (and here, I'm using the word 'hits' to refer to any contact between the message and the audience). However there are a few disadvantages to using ME as the focus of your efforts. The tables below illustrates the key differences between IM and ME:

Table 2: Comparison of Marketing Everywhere and Internet Marketing.

	Marketing Everywhere	Internet Marketing
Delivery Platform	Anything anywhere can be a mechanism of delivery, for example, you can sell your forehead as advertising space on eBay	Online media – social networks, mobile apps, websites, email marketing, banner advertising, adwords, tweets, blogs, online videos, content marketing
Audience	Very high	Potentially very high if not targeted

	Marketing Everywhere	Internet Marketing
Targeting	Generally very low, difficult to target individual sectors of the population	Potentially very high. Targeted ad campaigns have the power to directly connect with customers who have already bought your products
Conversion Rates	Extremely low.	Variable – depends on the product and the type of marketing.
Customer Tracking	Not available. Having a disparate marketing strategy makes tracking views and shares very difficult	Being able to track what customers are looking for is a lot easier. Tools like Google Analytics (covered in the chapter "Practically perfect SEO – measuring success") give you the power to pinpoint what your customers are looking at on your website.

	Marketing Everywhere	Internet Marketing
Cost	Generally high – printing 10,000 leaflets to put on car windows is more expensive than posting a link on a website	Generally low – unless you are using paid advertising, which can be very expensive for certain highly competitive industries, eg insurance

8.3 Ephemeral Marketing

Would I recommend using IM or ME? Well as an internet marketeer, you probably already know the answer to that one. ME does have its place, but one of the biggest problems with ME is the ephemeral nature of the message. For example, a few weeks ago I was thinking about getting some work done on my house and I saw a van go past with the name and number of a builder. I thought to myself 'ooh I must remember that number' and in the space of about 5 minutes I'd got distracted by something else and the thought was gone forever.

Now that marketing message managed a 'hit' but the hit did not turn into a conversion because the message was lost almost instantly. With online marketing, you can generally save or retrieve the links at a more convenient time.

As a side note, it is worth mentioning that some marketeers have coined the phrase 'ephemeral marketing' for a type of digital marketing that has a very short lived effect. Snapchat which displays an image or message for a very short length of time is a good example of ephemeral marketing. When posting a picture on Snapchat, you define how many seconds the recipient will be able to view the image before it is erased from their phone. Ephemeral marketing is useful for creating brand awareness or driving a specific market action like instantly viewing a trailer for an upcoming film, but for businesses that require repeat customers, or for businesses where people tend to shop around a lot before buying, ephemeral marketing is a less valuable tool.

Chapter 9 Social Media Marketing

9.1 Harnessing the power of Social Media

There's no getting away from the fact that if you want to succeed in online marketing today, you are going to have to use social media. The explosion of social media in a very short space of time has granted opportunities to engage with customers like never before. According to a report by We Are Social (http://wearesocial.net/blog/2015/01/digital-social-mobile-worldwide-2015/), by the end of this year, it is estimated that a third of the entire population of the world will be using social media. In the UK and the US over half the population already use social media.

So with over half your customers using social media, there is no excuse why you should not be using it.
Many business owners are reluctant to engage in social media for fear that they might get negative reviews, or someone will post nasty things about their company. There are two reasons why you should not be afraid of this: firstly, if someone has had a bad experience of your services, social media gives you the medium to listen to people, and the opportunity to deal with the issues that the client has had. Generally people don't complain about minor things but will tell everyone they know that they have had a bad experience (usually on Facebook and twitter), so you never actually hear what the negative views are directly. Making yourself accessible via twitter or Facebook will not only give you a chance to identify and rectify any issues, but will also make others see that you care about the service you give and make an effort to help customers.

Secondly, if someone decides to make up stuff about you, or post unpleasant things (which is actually quite rare in social media) then you have a chance to reply to their accusations, and in a worst case scenario, you can delete their comments or even get the abusing account banned.

This chapter of the book will only cover the major social media channels, but there are many, many more than you can use. Some channels are geared to specific industries- a few examples are:

1. ishade.com – accounting industry
2. linkedFA.com – finance and insurance
3. achitizer.com – architects
4. glozal.com – real estate agents
5. tankchat.com – oil and gas industry
6. sermo.com – us based physicians
7. lawyrs.net – guess which one this is
8. researchgate.net – scientists

There are also quite a few for computer programmers and software engineers (unsurprising really). If you work in a particular industry, or your customers come primarily from that industry, then it might be worth looking in to the relevant social media channels to see what opportunities are available to you there.

9.2 LinkedIn

As a bare minimum your company should have a LinkedIn page. This enables you to create business networks with customers, suppliers and affiliates, but also gives your business a better online reputation. Sometimes you will find connections that lead to exciting new business opportunities from unexpected sources here. LinkedIn is also very helpful when it comes to finding freelancers and contractors to carry out short term contracts.

You should create a personal LinkedIn profile and populate it as much as possible with information specific to your business before you create your company page. This means that when people look at your business page, they will find that there is a real person behind the business, learn a little bit about the person, and increase their trust of the brand. In the description for your personal profile, try to drop in a few keywords so that your profile will show up in the LinkedIn search results. In your personal profile, rather than list what you jobs you have done, try to list achievements and accomplishments, for example instead of "I have worked for 3 companies in the past which were all sold" you could write "I have participated in the successful business exit of 3 high value companies".
The summary section is also a good place to tell people about yourself as a person and what you can offer. This is where you can show what makes you unique and desirable as a business contact.

To create a LinkedIn page for your business, you need to log in to your personal page, then hover over 'interest' in the top bar and click on 'companies'. Then in the right hand side click on the 'create' button under the 'create a company page' heading. Once created, you should fill out the profile with a company description, company size, website URL, address and phone details. You can add posts on your company page to engage a wider audience and attract more followers.

Note: you cannot create a company page with a Hotmail or Gmail address. You will need to use a company email address. After you have completed both your personal and company pages, it's time to go wabbit huntin' (in the words of Elmer Fudd). The quickest method is to go to the search tool at the top and search for your industry type with your country, e.g., if searching for cosmetic surgery clinics, put in 'cosmetic surgery UK' then click the search button. Refine your search afterwards by clicking on your country in the right hand side. This will bring up a shedload of connections that you can potentially engage with. There's no harm in clicking on the follow button on the companies, and maybe clicking through to the employees page to see if you can connect with the people who make the purchasing decisions.

9.3 Facebook

The second vital ingredient in your social media cake is Facebook. Facebook allows people to interact with your business, and you can use it to publish regular updates and offers.

Setting up a your Facebook page

If you are new to Facebook, it can take a while to get used to. Since it's launch in February 2004, FaceBook has constantly evolved to try to compete with the other social media networks and encourage people to move away from them (remember Friendster and Myspace?). It has now evolved to the point where there are so many options and features that you can actually get courses on how to use it. (If you are interested, you can also take a masters degree in Facebook at the University of Salford). Starting out on Facebook is a steep learning curve, so here are a few pointers to get you started:

If you are a business then you will need a 'Facebook page' not a personal profile. Facebook pages share some features with personal profiles but they also include things like branding, analytics and advertising tools. Until a couple of years ago, you could create Facebook pages without requiring a personal account login, however the system has since changed so now you have to first create a personal account. This personal profile does not need to be explicitly linked to the business page so you can just create a personal account without filling in much information and then add a business page. Although it is better to create a full personal profile and use that in conjunction with the business page. As with LinkedIn, having a personal profile in tandem with a business page generates more trust with consumers and can be used to engage on a more personal level if required.

When making your Facebook business page, try to keep the name short. This will help if you decide to create ads in the future because the headline space in Facebook ads is limited to 25 characters. Once you have created a Facebook page, you cannot change the name of the page if it has more than 200 likes. It's also helpful to have a short name when it comes to creating a custom Facebook web address.

Facebook allows you to create a custom web address (aka vanity url) so when you send the link to your Facebook page, instead of looking like www.facebook.com/pages/my-business/857469375913?ref=ts it will look like www.facebook.com/mybusiness. You can choose any vanity url as long as it is not already taken. Make sure you get it right first time though because you can only change your vanity url once, if you need to change it after that, you will have to set up a whole new Facebook page and start over, and you won't just be able to move your followers across to the new one.

When creating your business page, exploit the 'about' section to fill in as much information as you can, including website address, contact details, company address, services, products, and links to specific pages on your site. For example, if you have a careers page on your site, you can add a paragraph about how great it is to work for your company and a link to your current vacancies page saying 'join us'. The text in this section is indexed by google so try to include your brand name a few times along with a healthy sprinkling of keywords. If you have a price list, this can be included here, either as plain text, or maybe as a downloadable pdf.

Mobile users get to see a shortened version of your description, the 'short description' field in your about page. Desktop users get to see the long version so it's a good idea to make sure both these fields are fully populated. Get your web address at the top of each one to ensure that people will have a chance to see it.

In both description fields make sure you get call to actions in there, maybe "give us a call today" or "check us out now". Keep the call to actions quite short and punchy. You can also add discount codes or special offers as a reward for clicking on the link.

Include a company mission field in your 'about page' – this will let people know what the focus of your business is, and gain some insight into the business culture you try to foster. Again, this is a chance to include some relevant keywords.

Adding a call to action button

After you have squeezed every bit of marketing juice out of the about page, it's time to add a call to action button. In the top area, you'll see a button labelled 'create call to action'. Click on it and you'll see a popup where you can configure this button. You have a limited number of options in the button types, including 'book now', 'contact us', 'use app', 'play game', 'shop now', 'sign up' and 'watch video'. Then you can enter a URL for the button to go to and an optional url for the mobile version if different. Click next and you get the option of adding an app link for iOS and Android devices. Leave them set as 'website' if you don't have an app for your business. Once created, you will be able to see how many clicks this call to action button has generated in the right hand side of your page (your visitors won't be able to see this information). Mouse over the box and a popup will appear showing you a graph of how many people have clicked on your call to action button in the last week.

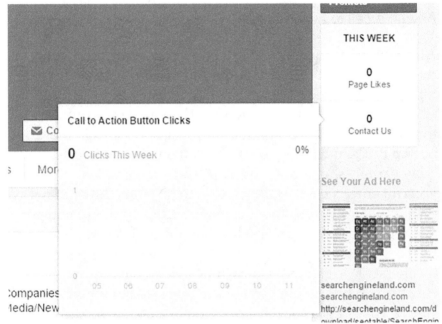

Fig 21: Call to action click stats in Facebook

Profile Picture and Cover design

Your profile picture should be recognisable when displayed in a small size, so avoid using text in this image. A company logo (or part of it) usually works ok. This image will be seen on all news feeds and anywhere your page is mentioned on Facebook. The image is resized to 180 x 180px when uploaded and displayed as 160 x 160 pixels, but the small version is only 43 x 43 pixels. Ideally you should upload any square image larger than 180 x 180 and let Facebook resize it down. Do not try to upload any image that is not square as this can get distorted.

When uploading a profile picture to your Facebook page, you can add a text description with the image. This is another opportunity to add call to actions and links to your website. You can also include the click bait elements from the description field above, i.e. offers, discount codes, etc.

The cover image is the larger image that sits in the background at the top of your profile page. As with the profile picture, you can add a description which will appear when people hover over your photo, and will appear when people click on your cover image. If you want to attract followers, give them some incentive here, e.g. "subscribe to this page to be the first to hear about new products and get secret discount codes available only to Facebook followers".

If you want, you can upload more than one cover image and rotate them regularly. This will push notifications to users to showcase your products with little effort on your part. The format of your cover picture will be displayed as 851px x 315px on desktops and resized down on smaller platforms, so you should try to upload an image at least 851px wide. You can reposition the image if it is too tall.

Apps and Tabs

One last thing to mention when setting up a new business page is that Facebook allows you to add extra tabs on your page. These tabs can contain 'apps' like event listings or competitions. To add an app, type the name of the app in the search bar at the top, something like "google map tab" or "photo contest app" then click on the app page. In the app page itself there will be a button to add the app to your pages tabs. You can even add third party apps like an ecommerce app (such as ecwid.com) so you can sell products on Facebook, or an app for booking appointments.

Sharing content?

So now you have your Facebook page all set up and optimised, what's next? As I said earlier, Facebook is a hugely powerful platform and to go through all the features would be beyond the remit of this book. If you want to explore Facebook to further exploit its features, it's worth viewing a few video tutorials on YouTube. However what you need to concentrate on next is getting people to like your page. The first thing you need to do next is make sure you get your Facebook buttons on your website or blog. Add both 'like' and 'share' buttons on your pages in an easy to find place.

Generally immediately after the content, or near the top of the page (or both if you can get away with it). If your web design allows it, having tabs at the edge of your site works really well as they are easy to find but unobtrusive. If you have products on your website, you will need to add buttons right next to the product description if possible. You can either get the embed code directly from Facebook, or I prefer to use www.sharethis.com which has a nice widget that you can use to put the share buttons on your site (and you can use it for free).

Free is good. We like free.

When using share buttons, Facebook will automatically select the first image on your page to include in the shared post, but you can help this along by adding meta tags to tell Facebook which image to use when sharing this page. The metatag looks something like this:

```
<link rel="image_src" type="image/jpeg"
href="http://mywebsite.com /myimage.jpg" />
```

Sometimes this tag doesn't work, so it's worth also adding an og:image meta tag like this:

```
<meta property="og:image"
content="http://mywebsite.com /myimage.png" />
```

You can also customise the text that appears in the facebook sharer app by adding more meta tags like this:

```
<meta property="og:title" content="Custom title goes here" />
<meta property="og:description" content="this
subtext appears under the title" />
```

And you can specify the link url too like this:

```
<meta property="og:url" content="
http://mywebsite.com /mypage.html" />
```

It is possible to add code to the sharing button to do that same thing as the meta tags, but it is better to have them in the page in case people just paste the url of your page into a Facebook post without using the share buttons.

Once you have added sharing buttons on your site you should start adding news stories and fresh content, and tell everyone about it using your share buttons. Facebook now allows larger thumbnail sizes so get some attractive images on there. People like sharing stories better when they have a funny caption, or the image is really interesting to them. You should also be proactive in liking other people's pages that you think might be interested in your services. This is especially useful if you have a B2B business.

Facebook hashtags

When adding posts, you should add relevant hashtags. This is a feature Facebook stole from Twitter, but is less commonly used. Clicking on hashtags will show people recent posts relevant to that topic, so if you can post messages relevant to recent news events, then more people are likely to see your post. Look out for what's trending on Facebook (shown in the right hand side of the site normally) for inspiration.

You can use your company name in hashtags, then you can link to these posts in your blogs and business cards and marketing materials. When you add hashtags to posts, you can display all posts with this tag by going to www.facebook.com/hashtag/mycompanyname which show up all posts containing #mycompanyname. You can even go further and give individual employees in your company their own hashtag e.g. #MykeAtBlackbox or something similar. Then these people can put that link on their business cards.

If you really need to get a bigger audience fast, then there is not getting away from it, you will have to pay for advertising. This is covered in the next chapter.

Facebook competitions

Competitions are a great way to get yourself noticed. Create a competition with an attractive prize and require people to share your post in order to win a prize. This virtual word of mouth effect will spread your brand awareness across Facebook quite quickly. It can also encourage people to like your Facebook page so giving you more followers. Having people follow you is like having their email address for email marketing. It means that if you post anything to your company page, it will pop up on all your followers news feed. So your primary aim on Facebook should be to try and get as many likes as possible.

Reciprocal Advertising and Cross Promotions

If you have a related business with a local supplier, you can set up reciprocal advertising. On your Facebook page you can advertise a link to your partner's business and they set up a link back to your business. This is similar to traditional link exchange schemes (covered in an earlier chapter of this book) but you can extend that further to create cross promotional activities. Say for example you had a bike shop. You could make a deal with the newsagent next door for a free copy of cycling weekly when you spend £10 or more in your bike shop, or you could make a deal with the sports shop around the corner so they give customers a £20 off voucher for your shop if they spend £40 on sports equipment in their shop.

This type of advertising works really well with social media because both businesses can use the same promotion to reach a much larger audience than they would be able to do just using their own followers.

Avoid click baiting

You've probably seen the adverts "This video totally blew my mind" or "I couldn't believe my eyes when I saw this" or "You won't believe what happens next..." This type of social media marketing is called 'click baiting'. The word "click baiting" used to be used to describe a legitimate form of SEO in which people were encouraged to visit your site based on the call to action and the relevancy of the content. Now it's generally used in a more pejorative way to describe these sorts of low value links with outlandish or cryptic claims in the headlines.

There are other types of click bait around which are of equally poor status, these are:

"10 things you didn't know about…" or "20 celebrities who" - these are called 'listicles'.

"I'll never look at a carrot in the same way again" - cryptic titles which give you no idea what the meaning is.

"60 million people can do this, can you?" - challenging title, with a bit of cryptic thrown in

"This woman talks about why she refused cancer treatment (and it's not what you think)" – self-undermining title.

After a while of being on social media (and clicking on these sorts of click baits) you usually get to the point where you assume that these sorts of links contain nothing worth reading, so people get tolerant of them. Not only does click baiting make people less likely to click on your page, it also means that the clicks you do get will be of very low quality and will make you look like you're desperate for traffic, so may damage your online reputation. Therefore, avoid click baiting or using ads or posts with headlines similar to click baiting.

Getting personal

Your Facebook fans are valuable, but they are also real people. So if you get a question from one of them, you should try to answer in a personal way. This can be done using 'mentions'. Mentions are a means of linking a person's profile in your Facebook post. To do this, put an @ symbol in front of their name when writing the reply. When you do this, a drop down menu will appear underneath and if you select their name in the dropdown, Facebook automatically puts their name as a link. When their name is 'mentioned' in a post, this will send the person a notification that they were mentioned and may also put that on their wall depending on their privacy settings. You can shorten the name to use just their first name by putting your cursor just after the surname and pressing backspace. Using first names makes it more informal and personal.

If you are replying to a post, you can also add your own name as a link. This is especially useful if there are multiple people who are admins on the account.
When posting to Facebook, use the word 'we' and 'our' to talk about your fans. This gives them a sense of community, for example "We now have 500 fans, thanks for all your support guys" or "Have a look at our newest fan of the month, Jennifer!"

Audience Research

One of the great things about Facebook is that you don't just get to tell people stuff about yourself, but you also find out really useful information about your target audience. When someone becomes a fan of your page, you get to see things like what films they like, what music they listen to, what other interests they have, and what other Facebook pages they have liked. You could do this with individual accounts to get ideas on possible promotion strategies, or you can use Facebook to get more representative information.

Until recently, Facebook search was able to show demographic information by using search queries like 'fans of x that like y' or 'fans of my page that are women' but this to no longer possible. Instead, in May 2014 Facebook launched its powerful new tool call Audience Insights.

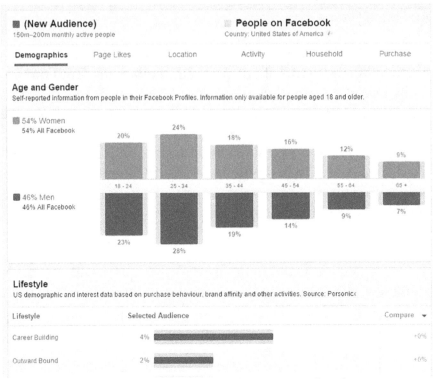

Fig 22: Audience Insights on Facebook

This is a fantastic tool that lets you see information about your fans including demographics, interests, location, activity, home ownership, purchase behaviour, education level, job area and more. You can filter this information by age, gender, interests, connections, and more advanced filters such as political leanings or life events.

This tool can tell a lot about your Facebook followers, but you can also use this tool for general research on the demographics of Facebook.

Another trick you can use is to put your competitor's page into insights so you can see the demographics of your competitors. This can be very handy if you want to target those customers more keenly.

To access Facebook Audience Insights, go to
https://www.facebook.com/ads/audience_insights then select
either 'everyone of Facebook' or 'people connected to your
page' in the popup to start. Note, you need more than 1000
likes to view demographic data on your own page.

Frequency and format of posts

Research has also found that the best time to post on Facebook
is 8pm to 12pm on a Wednesday or Sunday, and posting once
or twice a day leads to 40% higher user engagement. Posting
more than 4 times a day results in a decrease in engagement
due to over-crowding user's news feeds.

Posts with less than 80 characters in length receive 66% higher
engagement than longer posts and concise posts of around 40
characters have the highest engagement levels.

'Question' posts generate more than double the amount of
comments than statement posts, so if you want to engage user
interaction and get fans talking to each other, then posting a
question is a good way of doing this.

When posting offers, it has been shown that using the phrase
"£ off" is much more effective than "% off". Customers prefer
to avoid doing maths so knowing the real world value of an
offer is much more successful than the % value offer (even
though % off may actually save more money for the
consumer).

The most effective posts contain a short description with a
single images. Status-only posts also generate higher
engagement. Try to avoid more complex posts like those with
multiple links, thumbnail photos and videos.

9.4 Twitter

Some people love it, some people hate it, and some people just don't get it. That's how most people feel about Twitter. As a social media platform it's one of the new kids on the block having been around since 2006. Twitter was listed on the stock market in sept 2013.

Setting up your Twitter account

Setting up a twitter account is relatively straightforward. To start off building an optimised profile you should do the following steps:

1. **Select a great twitter name.**
   Generally this should be your brand name or something equally applicable. Try to keep your username short, simple and memorable. This username will form part of your twitter url, and will be included on your marketing material, so if you want to use 'free therapists' as your username, just be aware that it might also be read as 'free the rapists' (@freetherapists). Twitter will allow you to change your username as often as you like if you decide you need to, but try to avoid this as it can affect marketing materials and backlinks.

2. **Write a great bio.**
   Your 160 character twitter profile will probably appear quite high up when people search for your brand name, so your bio is very important. Include who you are,

what you do and why people should follow you in this bio. If you are setting up a company twitter account (which in contrast to Facebook and LinkedIn does not differ in any way from a personal account) it's useful to include the name of the person managing the account as this makes it more personal. You can also include your company website URL in the bio if you have space. Try to keep the bio informal and fun to reflect Twitter's conversational nature.

3. **Use an effective profile image.**
   Your profile picture will appear everywhere on twitter (and outside twitter in embedded feeds) so it's important that the image reflects your company. It does not always have to be a logo, it can be an object representative of your company, for example, a bike wheel, or maybe even a photo of the person managing the account. Twitter profiles with the default avatars are generally viewed as less trustworthy. To update your profile image, click on 'edit profile' at the right hand side of your profile page and then click on your image which should say 'change your profile photo' on the top of it. Your profile image should be 400 x 400px.

4. **Add a header image.**
   In 2014, twitter added the ability for people to add custom header images to their profiles. This is a large 1500 x 500 image that goes across the width of the page. You can use this image to add iconography, or a relevant photo or even include text in the image. Whatever you add will not be visible to mobile phone

users (which makes up the majority of Twitter). The procedure to change your header image is similar to changing the profile image but instead of clicking on your photo, just click on the 'add a header photo' link in the top centre area.

And that's all you need to do to get started. Twitter is a lot simpler and more streamlined than other social networks and takes very little time to learn. The hardest thing you need to learn is how to communicate your messages in less than 160 characters.

Future of Twitter

In May 2015, Twitter had more than 500 million users, over half of which are active users. However growth in Twitter has not kept up with investor expectations and on June 10 2015, its CEO Dick Costolo stepped down. This leaves Twitter's future direction uncertain. Apparently they are working on a curated news experience to try to engage "casual and unregistered users" called 'project lightning'.

Project lightning is designed to address one of the 2 fundamental flaws in twitter (the other being the low revenue on mobile advertising). The problem is that using Twitter is a very immediate experience with no short term memory. In other words, using Twitter is a bit like having a conversation with a dog using a dog translator. You cannot ask questions like 'what happened yesterday' or 'why did you just salivate at hearing that bell?' because it won't be able to tell you. It will just sit looking at you blankly wagging its #tail. All you can do is find out what people are saying now. This can give you the feeling that you've just walked into the middle of a conversation without knowing what the conversation is about. So to engage people using twitter you need to use messages that do not relate to previous knowledge. Assume everyone has just joined the conversation.

9.5 Google+

Google+ was Google's attempt at taking on Facebook in the social media space. Originally, it was designed to be a simpler social network. Google introduced the concept of 'circles' so you could assign contacts to different circles such as 'close friends' or 'work contacts' (or whatever you want the circle to be called) and then when you post content to Google's network, you can select which circles this post should be available to. This is a great concept as it allows you to use the same social media account for several different purposes. You can use it for work to let your work colleagues know that you are going to be meeting with a client this afternoon, and also for friends to invite them all out for a drink at the weekend. Contacts can be allocated to more than one circle, so your brother who works in accounts can be in 'friends', 'relatives', 'work contacts' and 'people who like star wars' circles.

Unfortunately, google+ never did get the momentum it deserved and its market share of social network users were mainly constrained to google employees and techies who appreciated the elegance of the system. It never really caught on with the mass market because it tried to be both a social networking tool and a business networking tool at the same time. So business users were put off by the social aspect and stuck to LinkedIn and social users were put off by the lack of social features so stuck with Facebook.

Google originally decided to integrate google+ with its other products including google business, effectively pitting it against LinkedIn in the business networking sphere. This again didn't really make much headway, and when Google plus's chief architect, Vic Gundotra left the company in April 2014, it was pretty much described by industry watchers as 'walking dead'. Despite Google's denial that the product was still alive, few updates have been made to it, and more recent product launches such as Google Photo are no longer chained to Google+. You don't even need a google+ account to log into YouTube anymore and google hangouts has stopped requiring google+.

Therefore, it is unlikely that any social marketing time put into Google+ will be worth the effort. We've even stopped adding the google plus share button on websites because they just weren't getting clicked on.

9.6 Instagram

27.6% of the adult population of the US used Instagram in 2015. There are many image sharing networks, but Instagram (owned by Facebook) is the biggest, with 200 million active users. It's one of the 10 more popular smartphone apps – which is probably why Facebook paid so much for it: $1 billion.

The chart below shows the 10 most popular smartphone apps for 2014.

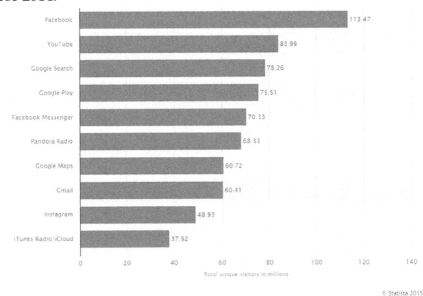

© Statista 2015

Show further information   Show sources information

Fig 23: Top smartphone apps in 2014 ranked by monthly visitors (in millions)

source: http://www.statista.com/statistics/250862/unique-visitors-to-the-most-popular-mobile-apps-in-the-us/

Instagram was the 9th most popular app in 2014 with 48 million users - not bad considering it was only launched in October 2010.

Using image sharing networks can get you access to certain demographics that are harder to reach on other networks. Studies suggest that 90% of people on Instagram are under 35 years old, and 68% of them are female. This makes it a good platform to advertise jewellery, fashion, and entertainment. A disproportionate amount of these have high income brackets.

Getting started on Instagram

To start using Instagram, you will need the app. There's a version for iOS, Windows 10 mobile and Android and there are also third party versions for blackberry and other niche mobile platforms. The mobile app is used to upload, edit and share images – you cannot do this using a desktop PC or Mac. If you are using a desktop, you can only view images, add comments and share content.

Once you have downloaded the app, you need to register and set up your profile. You can make your profile private if you want to spend some time playing with it before making it public. As with twitter accounts, you get a profile image and a short bio, in this case 150 characters. Your profile picture should be the same as your twitter and Facebook profile pictures to maintain consistency across social media platforms.

Because Instagram is a relatively basic platform, you need to connect to your other social media accounts to get the best out of it. Go to profile tab > edit sharing settings then choose which networks you wish to connect to. Each time you upload a photo (or video) you can select which network to make the photo appear in.

Using Instagram for your business

Instagram has a particular culture which means that you won't see hundreds of blurry or tiny images. Content creators are proud of their uploads, thanks in part to the image editing and photo filter tools included in the app. One of the core messages of Instagram is to 'find beauty everywhere'. Therefore, to get your pictures and videos shared and commented on, you need to create great looking content. For businesses, you need to portray how your company sees the world. This is not just uploading pictures of brand logos, products or staff members, you need to offer a view of the lifestyle that your products or services make possible. You need to show what gives you inspiration, even if it's an ancient tree in the middle of a field, or a pebble on a beach - as long as it reflects your company's vision, then it's a vision you can convey in pictures.

Think of Instagram as your mood board. What you want people to feel about your company is as important as what they think about your company.

Growing your audience

If you want to grow your audience, you need to create high quality, on-brand content that people will want to see in their Instagram feed. If you create interesting or popular content, this can also appear on non-followers' feeds via the 'explore' tab or the 'news' tab. Here are a few other tips to grow your audience:

- Add a link to your website footer for your Instagram account and make it available on every page

- Put the link on marketing materials and press releases. If you create a press release with images, make these images available on Instagram also

- Run photography competitions via Instagram. You should choose a relatively desirable prize like an iPad mini or an apple watch (remember your Instagram audience are quite tech savvy, and statistically have above average income so a 10 quid discount as Asda won't generate much interest).

- Announce your account on other social media platforms and link back to your profile page.

- Use photo captions to optimal effect by adding a description of the product, a call to action with URL or a question to spark debate on a relevant subject. Note, if you use a url in a caption, they are not clickable so try to make it short and memorable. If you want people to visit your website, you can also add a bit of text to say 'click on the link in our bio to read more'

- Use hashtags. Including hashtags can be a way to tap into a current theme, but avoid overuse of hashtags and this can make it look spammy- ideally no more than three to five per photo. Avoid general hashtags like #furniture or #food as they will get few people finding your content in there. Instead use more descriptive and creative hashtags like #mediterranianfood or #retrofurniture. Try looking at related businesses to yours and see what hashtags they are using. A few popular hashtags to use are #picoftheday, #instagood, #followme, #beautiful, #love, #tagsforlikes, #happy and #cute

- Use geo-targeting on your photos. Instagram allows you to geo-tag your photos with the location that they were taken. This is then added to a photo map so that people who are near to your location will see the pictures that were taken nearby (a bit like the 'people near me' feature of google plus). This can lead people to visit your shop if they are close by, or just to give them sense of where you come from.

- Share customer photos. This can be a really great tactic when running competitions - show competition winners holding up your product with a big grin on their faces, or people sitting on a bike they have just bought from your shop. Invite people to send in their pictures to you or search for you images with your products in by searching for your brand name. For example, Sharpie posts pictures of people's drawings made using sharpie pens.

- Add comments to other's postings. Perhaps thanking them for buying your product, or commenting on how good their picture is, will enable to get your name spread around and hopefully will attract some people to look at your pictures. Try to comment on images that either contain your products, or are in line with the mood board you are trying to create.

- Golden ticket tactic – this involves selecting a single follower and send them a surprise offer or gift. Select a follower that has lots of followers themselves and encourage them to share the news.

There are a few more ideas on the Instagram for Business website (https://business.instagram.com/) which includes case studies of successful marketing campaigns by the likes of Mercedes-Benz and Ben and Jerrys.

9.7 Automating social media

Keeping all your social media marketing up to date can be a lot of work if you have to monitor and update a dozen social media accounts with multiple posts per day. Generally the content shared on the networks will be the same, so having some sort of automation strategy will save you a lot of time and effort.

Thankfully, there are a quite a few options for keeping your social media updated - googling the phrase 'social media management tools' just got me 276 billion results. The choice of which tool you should use depends on your budget and which social platforms you need to support. The graph below summarises the market share of the major players in the market.

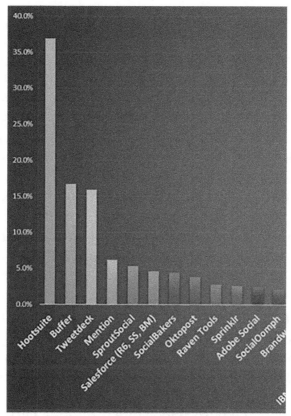

Fig 24: Most popular social media automation tools

Hootsuite

By far the most popular tool is Hootsuite. You can get started using Hootsuite for free if you only want to try it out. The free account lets you link up to 3 social media accounts and includes support for Facebook pages and LinkedIn company pages. To add Facebook pages, you have to link to your normal FB account first so its recommended that you add the facebook pages before any other social media accounts. You can remove your personal account after you've added the Facebook page to free up one of your 3 slots. The paid for accounts support up to 100 social profiles across different social networks so you don't have to worry about filling it up really.

Hootsuite has a very helpful tutorial that assists you in setting up your account and get you started using the system. Once you have your Hootsuite account up and running, you can then publish content to all your linked social media at once.

To add links in the posts, Hootsuite includes a URL shortener which convert them to http://ow.ly links. You could add links without the shortened version, but using the converted links will allow you to view analytics about how many clicks you got on each link and which network the clicks came from.

Another handy use for these kinds of tools is that many of them, including Hootsuite, support scheduled posts. If you wanted to schedule a post to appear alongside a media event, you just set the post up as normal and instead of clicking on 'send now' click on the calendar icon above it, then select what date and time you want the system to post the message for optimal impact.

Fig 25: Publishing new content in Hootsuite

To monitor social media activity, the system makes use of 'streams'. Streams are lists of posts that you might be interested in - so you could monitor any mentions of your company, or specific keywords or hashtags, then when you find any interesting posts, you can share these on your platforms or contact the individual who mentioned your company. Each stream can monitor up to 3 keywords, but you can have several streams running at once in different tabs. Setting up your streams takes a bit of work at first, so it's a good idea to have a clear idea about what streams should be monitored. For example, you could set up a tab that just looks at mentions for yourself, then maybe another tab with mentions of competitors, then maybe a 3rd tab for monitoring wider industry news.

After you have made a few posts using Hootsuite, you can view the statistics on engagement, and the system lets you create great looking reports. Some of the reports are not available in the free version, but there are enough of them to satisfy most marketing directors.

Hootsuite is a very powerful platform with a plethora of invaluable tools, but it does have some limitations. One of such is the fact that you cannot tag people in Facebook posts. You will have to go straight to Facebook to do this. Another is that you cannot easily select an image for a linked page. Again, you will have to go to the relevant social media account to do this.

Twitterfeed

If you already have a blog and want to automatically publish this content into your social media feeds then there is another great tool called Twitterfeed (twitterfeed.com) .This is a free service that reads your website's RSS feed, then automatically publishes that content to LinkedIn, Facebook and Twitter. The beauty of Twitterfeed is that you only have to set it up once and then you can forget about it. Most CMS systems automatically generate RSS feeds from blogs, and online blogging websites will also publish this, but if your blog does not create RSS feeds automatically, then you can use online services to create a feed. This is a bit more work than using automatic WordPress or blogger.com RSS generators, so if you have not already set up a blog, consider using those systems that publish RSS feeds.

Social Media Management tools can save you a lot of time if you do a lot of social networking with your business. If you are one of those businesses that shy away from social media, then you are missing out on a lot of potential clients. While you are avoiding Facebook and twitter, you can be sure that your competitors are already getting fans and followers.

Chapter 10. Online Advertising

Most online ads you see will be PPC ads. PPC stands for 'pay per click'. This form of advertising employed by most online advertising networks charges the advertiser a small amount each time someone clicks on their advert. PPC is used by Google, Yahoo and Bing. There are other forms of paid advertising such as pay per like (used in social media networks) or pay per conversion which is commonly used in affiliate marketing. These are also covered in this chapter.

10.1 Google AdWords

Google AdWords are by far the most popular form of online advertising. These ads appear in the search pages and affiliate networks in google, so have the potential to reach millions of people. The beauty of AdWords is that you already know what the viewer is interested in before they get shown your ad. So if someone searches for 'mountain bikes' you know that they have an interest in bikes so having your bike shop advert would be more interesting to them.

When you create an AdWords account, it will look quite complicated at first. Essentially all adverts are created as part of a 'campaign' and in each campaign you have one or more 'ad groups'. Each ad group targets a number of keywords and has one or more ads to display. You need to create more than one ad as the wording and text of the ad will make a difference to the number and quality of leads you get from it. AdWords automatically rotate your ads, and tweak the ratio so that the most successful ads are shown more often than lower performing ads.

Each campaign is allocated a daily budget. Google will then display your ads in rotation with all the other relevant ads in the search results until your budget has been spent. Generally the higher your budget, the higher your ad will appear in the search results, and therefore more likely to be clicked on. From experience, we know that ads at the higher positions have higher conversion rates. Lower ads are more likely to be visited by people who are not immediately interested in making a purchasing decision or enquiry, but are shopping around for information.

One of the dangers of AdWords is that if you do not optimise your campaigns you could be throwing a lot of money at advertising with very little benefit. You could hire an SEO company that is practiced at getting higher ROI for AdWords, and if you are planning on spending a lot of AdWords money this could be the better option. But if you want to do it yourself, you will need to spend time researching how to make the most of your ads and what keywords to target. Here are a few tips to improve your AdWords:

1. Use Captial Case In Your Ad – Capitalise The First Letter Of Each Word To Make It Stand Out More

2. If you sell a product, put the price in your ad: "All bike helmets only £20" for example. Online shoppers are quite impatient and having the price right there in front of them without having to do any extra effort or clicks is a time saver. Another benefit is if people are looking for bargains or have already found a price for the product elsewhere cheaper, then they will not use up your clicks. This is especially true if you are selling high value and luxury items. People looking for £10 imitation Rolex watches won't click on an ad that has a $1000 price tag.

3. Use negative keywords to filter out timewasters. Negative keywords are keywords that you can add to an advert to exclude your ad from searches including this keyword. Keywords such as 'sale', 'imitation', 'fake', 'ex display' and 'knock off' are good to exclude if you are selling genuine designer products.

4. Use the correct currency for the country – if you sell internationally, create a separate ad for each currency region with the correct currency in it.

5. Google ads have a very limited character length. The headline is limited to 25 characters maximum, the URL is limited to 35 characters (although that's only the url shown on the page, the actual url can be much longer). The description beneath can only be 35 characters for each line. And you only get 2 lines. So you need to squeeze as many call to action and keywords in there are you can.

6. Check out your competitors ads. Chances are they have spent years fine tuning their ads to make the most out of them. Why not take a short cut and copy what they have done.

7. Include a call to action in the headline – try to be creative with CTAs – 'buy online' or 'download now' won't improve your click rate, but something like 'Try A Refreshing Smoothie Today' will be more successful.

8. Include a special offer – everyone likes offers. "£10 off New Bikes" works better than "10% Off New Bikes" – even if the bikes are worth £200 which means the % deal will save you twice as much! Free shipping is a particularly effective offer, as studies have shown it to increase conversions by more than 50%.

9. Instead of saying how great you are, tell customers how you can help them. So in place of "Our bike helmets are amazing" use "You'll look amazing in our helmets".

10. Add a sense of urgency. If you add phrases like 'limited stock', 'Sale ends boxing day' or 'Only 4 left in stock' then this motivates people to click on your ad now. This does mean you might have to update your ads more often, but will also give you higher click rates.

11. Reduce risk – add phrases like '14 day return', 'secure payment processing' and 'price guarantee' to increase people's confidence in buying from you – this is more important if you are not a well-known company.

12. Make the headline and first description a full sentence. If the ad appears at the top of the search results, it will display your headline and first line of description as a single sentence. This can only happen if you put a punctuation mark at the end of your first description line, for example:

£25 Off All Mountain Bikes
When You Order Before March 20th!
Free Online Delivery In The UK

Will turn into:

£25 Off All Mountain Bikes - When You Order Before March 20th!
Free Online Delivery In The UK

13. Include the main keywords – when the ad is shown in response to a search containing this keyword, the keyword will appear in bold and thus make it stand out a little bit more. You can include the keyword in headline, description and display URL.

14. Avoid trademarked names – these can get your ad rejected. Google has an automatic trademark filter so if you put 'coke cola' in your ad, chances are it will get rejected straight away.

15. Customise your display URL – the URL text can work as a call to action. If you click on the display URL, you

do not necessarily go to that URL, as the real URL is defined separately. Try out urls like 'mysite.com/bikevouchers', or 'mysite.com/freetrial' or even 'mysite.com/secretsale' which works well as people thing they are getting to a part of the website that they would not normally be able to visit.

16. Use Ad extensions. These are ways of adding extra information to ads. One example is the location extension which will display your businesses address, phone number and a map link. This makes your ads more prominent and takes up more page space. Most ad extensions are free to set up, but some aren't such as the call button for the 'call extension', or the download button of an 'app extension'.

17. Get stars on your ads. Encourage people to leave reviews for you on sites like trustpilot.com and then you will see ratings stars appearing on your ads. Do not add your own fake reviews as this can get your site blacklisted from the reviews sites.

18. Keep testing and retesting your ads. If you create similar ads with small changes in the wording, you can compare the click rates to see which method gets more clicks and which method gets higher conversions per click. Keep tweaking your ads to build up your conversion rates.

10.2 Facebook Ads

Facebook advertising is another good way to increase your brand awareness and increase your online fan base. The main difference between AdWords and Facebook ads is that if someone engages with an AdWords ad, you have a very short time window to convert them into customers. If someone likes your Facebook page on the other hand, then you have the ability to continue marketing to them for as long as they stay liking your page. The exception here is if you are using some sort of customer lifecycle marketing system – see chapter 12 Customer Lifecycle Marketing for more information about how to do this.

Due to the way Facebook generates newsfeeds (based on user interaction), your page's posts will probably only reach about 5% of your audience unless you promote the post. Promoted posts will be visible by all your fans.

There are a few types of ad that you can place on Facebook:

1. Domain ad – this is the basic type which is displayed in the right hand column. You can enter a title, short description and URL. Clickthrough rates are quite low for these ads but they are the cheapest. Note, these ads don't appear on the mobile platform.

2. Page post link – These look like regular news feed posts except with a 'sponsored ad' text at the top. These have better performance than domain ads and have the added benefit of generating likes for your page. These ads appear on the mobile site, in the newsfeed and also

in the right hand column. You can use videos, photos or just plain old text in these ads.

3. Multiproduct – this is a relatively new type of ad (introduced in June 2014) that allows you to put up to 3 products in a showcase. These do not appear in the right hand side but are available on mobiles.

4. Unique Engagement ad – these are special ads that require at least £30,000 spending to get started.

When you create an ad, you should set out from the start what goal you want to achieve. Do you want more likes? Or more click-throughs to your website? Or do you want more conversions? The goal will define the type of ad you use. Conversions are far more valuable than website clicks so it's advisable to use this instead of clicks unless you are just getting started and need to increase your like count. There are other types of goals that you can define, the illustration below shows these options:

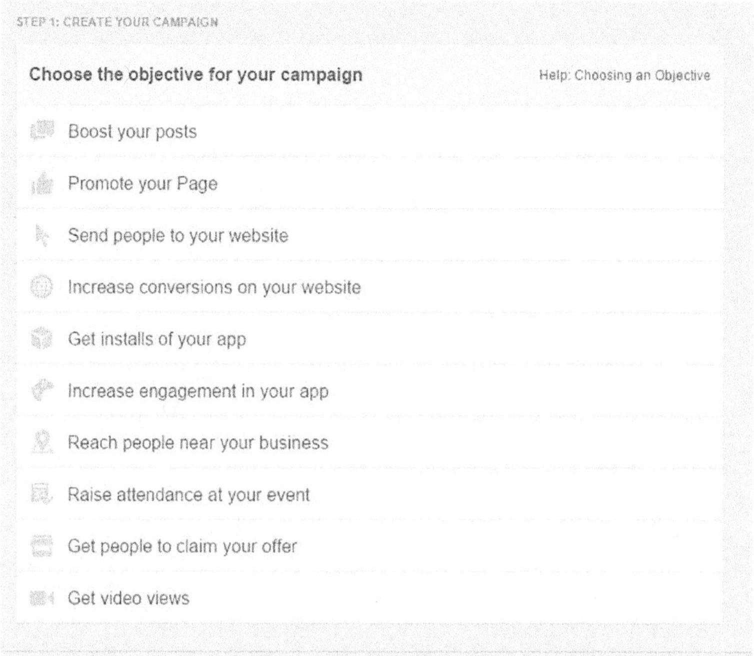
STEP 1: CREATE YOUR CAMPAIGN
Choose the objective for your campaign
Help: Choosing an Objective
Boost your posts
Promote your Page
Send people to your website
Increase conversions on your website
Get installs of your app
Increase engagement in your app
Reach people near your business
Raise attendance at your event
Get people to claim your offer
Get video views

Fig 26: Campaign objectives for Facebook ads

One of the best things about Facebook ads is that you get the option of specifying a target audience. Since Facebook knows quite a lot about each user, this targeting is very successful.

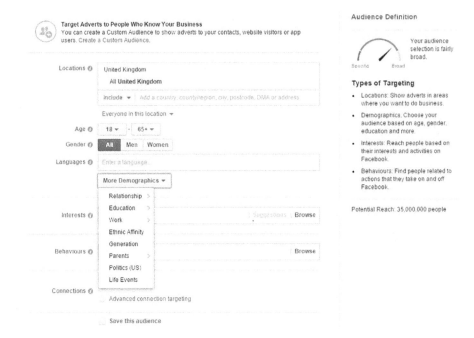

Fig 27: Target demographics for Facebook ads

After you have defined your advert, you can set a daily budget. Start off with £3 per day just to start off, you can increase this limit later. The estimated daily reach for a 'clicks to website' advert on £3 per day is 1,200 – 3000 people. Note you won't get this many website visitors, this is just an estimation of how many times your ad will appear. Generally Facebook ads have a click through rate (CTR) of about 0.04% to 0.05% on average if placed in the right hand column.

Adverts placed in the newsfeed have much higher CTRs of between 1% and 7% depending on the quality of the ad and the target audience. So if you have an ad in the main news feed, a budget of £3 per day will probably give you about 10-15 website visits per day. Mobile news feed ads tend to have higher CTRs than desktop news feed ads.

After you have set your budget, you have the option of adding an image or multiple images. Until recently this image was one that needed to be uploaded to your Facebook profile, but now Facebook gives you the option of adding stock images. To add stock photography images, just click on the 'professional images' button in the 'select images' section and a popup will appear that allows you to search the massive Shutterstock photography library for a suitable image.

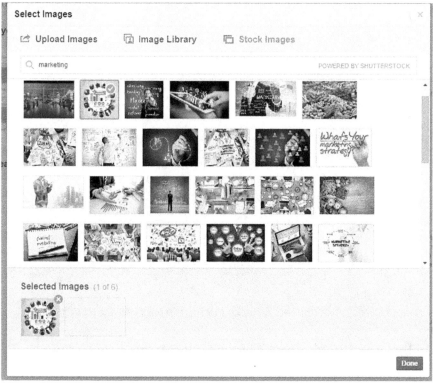

Fig 28: Adding stock photography for Facebook ads

Then all you have to do is edit the text and links for the advert and add a call to action button (optional).

Run the ad for a week and then measure your ad's performance using the Adverts Manager. To access this, click on the arrow at the top right corner of your profile and select 'Manage Adverts'.

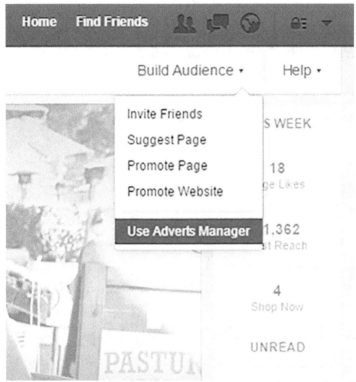

Fig 29: Accessing the Adverts Manager in Facebook

In the Adverts Manager you can get reports of how many people your ad has reached and how they have responded to it.

If you would like more detailed statistics, you can integrate your ads with Google Analytics. Facebook provides a very useful guide on doing just that here:
https://www.facebook.com/business/google-analytics/

It's a bit technical doing this but it does give you much greater insight on who is clicking on your adverts.

We advise that you review the ad's performance for at least a week, and possibly tweak the settings to get more value for money. Look at where your visitors are coming from, who they are, and what their interests are. If you find that most of your clicks come from a certain demographic, change the ad parameters to target this demographic specifically. Once you have tested out your advert and optimised the settings, you can then increase the budget to the required level.

We have found that using Facebook is an extremely effective medium, more so than Google AdWords, and is a lot easier to use than the AdWords system.

10.3 Affiliate Marketing

Wikipedia defines Affiliate marketing as
"A type of performance-based marketing in which a business rewards one or more affiliates for each visitor or customer brought by the affiliate's own marketing efforts."
Essentially, affiliate marketing is where you market someone else's products or services and get a cut of the revenue for each sale. There are 3 parties involved in affiliate marketing:

1. **Advertiser** – this is the company who sells products or services such as software, clothing, electronics, insurance, utilities etc.
2. **Publisher** – an individual or company who promotes and markets the advertiser's products or services in exchange for a commission or similar reward
3. **Consumer** – The people who buy the advertisers products via the publisher.

This sounds like an easy way to make money, and if you are good at it, then you can make a good living wage out of it. Most of the major online comparison and online voucher code websites run off an affiliate marketing structure. For example, if you are searching for the cheapest car insurance, you might want to use a comparison site which shows you prices for different packages and when you apply for the insurance, you are directed to the insurer's website. When you buy the insurance, the insurance company gives some money to the comparison website in return for your referral.

A publisher can advertise for more than once company, or can just sell products for a single company. Many companies run their own affiliate marketing scheme. You have probably seen the types of offers like 'recommend a friend and get 10% off next order' – this is a form of affiliate marketing which makes consumers into publishers effectively.

When using online affiliate marketing, generally publishers are required to include tracking information on their websites. This is normally in the form of tracking cookies, but can also be in the form of tracking urls. This allows the advertisers to know when a product is purchased and which affiliate it was that referred the purchaser.

Some publishers create specific websites with affiliate links to products, and then spend their time doing SEO in order to get more people to visit the publisher's website. Successful SEO marketers can use this tactic to get higher than the advertiser's website in the search engines, so leading more people to buy via them. This is quite a successful business model, but requires a lot of effort to reap the rewards.

Here are some tips for making money from affiliate marketing:

1. Choose your subject area carefully. This is one of the most important steps. Choose something that interest you and that you know a bit about. If you're a keen cyclist, set up a fan blog for cycling or a bike product review website.

2. Find a good affiliate program. It's worth shopping around to find the best program – choose one that includes products that you yourself would want to buy.

It's not always about having a high commission rate. 1% of 100 sales is better than 10% of 1 sale. If you are using one of the bigger affiliate programs like commission junction, linkshare or peerfly, look at whether you get a dedicated affiliate manager. You could also consider Amazon Associates which gives you 10% commission on each sale and has a vast array of products. Google used to do a very good one called Google Affiliate Network, but sadly this has been retired.

3. Create a community – use Facebook to connect to people who are likely to become customers.

4. Run a blog – Blogs are very successful in creating affiliate links, and search engines love sites which are focused, have good content and are regularly refreshed.

5. Stay focused – if you try to sell a diverse array of products you are likely to have a lower conversion rate. Stick to your core products and if you want to advertise other products, consider setting up another website to focus on those separately.

6. Avoid using PPC or other forms of advertising. Some publishers don't even have a website and just use AdWords – while this can sometimes get a positive ROI, you are more likely to lose money than make it because there will be other affiliate marketeers trying to do the same thing so you will end up in a bidding war for smaller returns.

7. Research your topic and generate unique content. Become an industry expert and people will trust your recommendations more.

8. Don't expect overnight success. Like SEO, affiliate marketing is a long ball game. You won't make much money at first, and you probably won't become a millionaire doing it (unless you have the capital to build up a massive comparison or review website).

Section 4 – Selling Online

Online shopping is a specialised industry. There are many thousands of online shops, most of which fail to turn over an operating profit. This section deals specifically with the challenges and opportunities that online commerce, or e-commerce faces.

Here at Blackbox E-commerce, we have over 10 years' experience of building and running ecommerce websites. From small clothing retailers to multi-national jewellery websites. Despite the variety of businesses and size of retailer, they all compete on a level playing field when it comes to online shopping. The size of your shop makes no difference online. The range and presentation of your products is far more important.

Read this section to find out more about how to become a successful online retailer.

Chapter 11 Ecommerce

Selling stuff online is not as easy as it looks. There are 2 main tasks that you have to master in order to become a successful online business: Getting visitors and converting visitors to customers.

The first task is achieved by SEO, online ads, social media marketing, and traditional marketing (print, magazine ads, TV ads, radio, etc.) The online marketing strategies are covered earlier in this book.

The second task is achieved by Conversion marketing. There is a fine art to increasing conversions. One that the big online stores have invested millions of dollars researching. Amazon didn't happen to use one-click ordering by chance. It was in response to years of testing and trailing different methods or payment procedure.

Your conversion rate is the measure of an ecommerce website's success. You might be getting thousands of visitors every day, but if your conversion rate is close to zero then you are losing out on a huge amount of revenue. Similarly, if you have a killer conversion rate of 50% but are only getting 2 people per day, then you are only going to make an average of one sale per day. What you need is a combination of ecommerce SEO and high conversion rates to hit the sweet spot.

11.1 Increasing conversion rates

Below are 7 things that you can do to improve your online sales. Some of these things relate to improving your conversion rate, and some of them are to increase your traffic through natural SEO and online marketing. The effect of each factor varies from website to website and each type of customer responds differently, so knowing your customers and your products is essential.

1. Keep it simple
The principle of Occam's razor should be applied to every step of your website. If people have one extra button to click or one extra form field to fill in, then this will erode your conversion rates. Some sites benefit from greater simplicity, for example, if you are selling just one product you don't need a multi-page ecom system with discount codes, customer registration, or shopping basket page. A simple one-page site with the product on it, a quantity field, information on returns and a big old PayPal button will do the job for you nicely.

2. Focus your landing pages
If you are using email marketing, PPC (pay per click) or offline marketing you need to create a landing page that is specific to that ad. For example, if you put an advert in a magazine, you should put in a unique URL that relates to the magazine - e.g. mydomain.com/magazinename - then make the landing page have the same copy as the advert, if possible put the logo of the magazine on the page and any products that appear in the ad. If you can put on a one-click buy button for these products that would be even better.

3. Your home page is the most important page of the site

Forget the shopping basket, shipping information or even product pages. If you want to maximise your click throughs, the home page is where you should concentrate most of your efforts. 90% of your web visitors will see this page first so it is essential that you put your best converting products on the front, and any products that are unique to your website. The homepage is like the shop front of a physical store. When you walk past a shop, you will see that they do a lot of work on getting the shop window looking as enticing as possible and having it looking fresh by regularly updating its shopfront.

4. Make your website load as quickly as possible

A slow website will bounce visitors like an inflatable castle, so you need to make sure that all pages load up in 3 seconds or less. Even if this means taking off that massive flash intro that you were so proud of. Another reason for having a fast loading site is that Google now uses site loading speed as part of its ranking algorithm, favouring faster loading sites over slower ones.

5. Show your credentials

People are wary of buying things from websites that they have not used before or that their friends have not used before, so the more you can do to convince people that you are an honest and reputable etailer, the better. If possible, have a physical address and landline phone number on your contact page. Include reviews and testimonials from real people (even if some of them are bad, it's better than not having any). Include an 'about us' or 'company history' type page.

DotComGiftShop sent me a great marketing email yesterday. At the bottom is a picture of the two ladies who run the website and a bit of information about the company and its ethos. This creates empathy with the brand and improves buyer confidence.

6. Get a freephone/toll free number
Not quite as important now as it used to be since a lot of people use their mobiles which are not free on 0800 / 1-800 numbers. Still, it's worth doing as it can make the difference between a sale and an abandoned shopping cart.

7. Check your website is free of spelling errors
A recent survey suggested that spelling errors can reduce your conversion rates by as much as 50%. So there's no excuse not to regularly check through your website to check for spelling mistakes.

11.2 Selling products on Amazon

If you want to sell your product on amazon.com it's really simple. All you need to do is set up an Amazon Seller Account to sell your items via the Amazon Marketplace. The Amazon Seller Account allows you to upload your products to Amazon's database using either an uploaded data file or you can use the Amazon Seller Desktop software to control you product and inventory.

The fee for selling on Amazon varies depending on the type of product you are selling, but typically you will have to pay between 10-20% of the item value in fees.

What if I want to sell on my own website?

There are two options if you want to use Amazon to sell via your own website:

1. Amazon Checkout

Amazon checkout allows you to use the Amazon payments ecom engine to power your own ecommerce website. This allows customers to log in to your site using their own amazon login, and their shipping and payment information stored in Amazon is used to carry out the purchase. You can either use your own ecom system to integrate into Amazon's API, or you can use Amazons system which uses a popup window to complete purchases

2. Amazon Webstore

An Amazon Services Europe Product

Amazon Webstore makes it quick and very easy to set up an ecommerce website. You can set the webstore up 'in a matter of minutes' according to their website - which in reality probably means a matter of hours, then a few more days messing around with it. You don't need any programming skills to set up a web store, and you can also enable the option to allow the same products to be displayed on Amazon's main website.

In the last few weeks, Amazon have announced that they are closing their webstore service, but will continue to support current merchants on the platform for a year until they find a suitable alternative. No reason has been given for this move.

Amazon Fulfilment
For the ultimate in fire-and-forget ecommerce, you can also register for Amazon Fulfilment. The way this works is that you set up your webstore or seller account, and then send your stock to the nearest Amazon warehouse. Amazon then takes care of all the shipping, order tracking, returns, customer queries and anything else that might get in the way of your busy day.

How much does it cost to sell via Amazon?

Having an Amazon Seller account is free if you choose to have an 'individual' account, but there is a charge of 75p per item sold. If you upgrade to the pro-merchant account, the monthly fee is £25.00 but the per-item fee is £0. Therefore you need to sell at least 34 items per month to benefit from the pro-merchant account.

In addition, you also have to pay a 'referral' fee. This fee varies depending on the type of product:

Table 3: Amazon referral fees per category

Categories	Referral Fee	Applicable Minimum Referral Fee (applied on a per-item basis unless otherwise noted)
	Amazon deducts the greater of the applicable referral fee percentage or applicable per-item minimum referral fee. See "Referral Fees" notes above.	
Amazon Device Accessories	45%	£0.40
Beauty	15%**	£0.40
Beer & Wine	12%	--
Books, Music, Videos, DVDs	15%	--
Car & Motorbike	15%**	£0.40
Clothing	15%**	£0.40
Computers	7%	£0.40
Computer Accessories	12%*	£0.40

Consumer Electronics (excl. accessories)	Individuals: 10%**	£0.40
	Pro-Merchant Subscribers: 7%**	£0.40
Electronic Accessories	12%*	£0.40
DIY & Tools	12%**	£0.40
Grocery	15%	--
Health & Personal Care	15%**	£0.40
Jewellery	25%**	£1.25
Large Appliances (with the exception of Accessories, Microwaves and Range Hoods)	7% **	£0.40
Musical instruments & DJ	12%**	£0.40
Software	15%	--
Spirits	10%	--

Tyres	10%**	£0.40
Video Games	15%	--
Video Game Consoles	8%	--
Watches	15%**	£1.25
Everything else	15%**	£0.40

The fulfilment charge is tiny when you think that you could spend more than that on petrol going to the post office and back never mind the hassle of having to organise deliveries and set it all up.

For a typical small ecom website shipping an average of 2 orders per day costing £30 per item it will cost £32.98 for the fixed costs plus £240 for selling fees and fulfilment. That means if a site is selling £1,800 per month, its ecom charges will be £273 which works out at about 15% in total - Sounds a bit high, but if you consider that you do not have to handle any of the delivery, returns, warehousing, fraud screening, customer enquiries and stock control it means your overheads are only 15% of the retail price. All you have to do is restock the warehouse when you run low and update the product information using the desktop software every so often.

If you wanted to buy a full spec ecommerce system (with or without Amazon integration), PCI DSS compliance, secure server and ongoing maintenance will cost you far more than this. Also, having SEO on your own ecom website to the level where you get a similar level of traffic as you would on Amazon would be incredibly expensive too.

Really if Amazon is this good for small to medium scale retailers, is there any reason to build your own ecommerce website?

11.3 VAT rules for UK Businesses

If you have a business based in the UK, for most people the tax system is relatively simple. Although if you sell digital products online, the EU rules on automated digital services may apply. Read on to find out what your tax situation is...

Should I be VAT Registered?

If you earned more than £81,000 in the last year (based on 2015 tax rates) you must be VAT registered. If you earn below this, you can still register for VAT, but the benefits of doing so will be limited. See this page for more information about UK domestic tax rates:
http://www.hmrc.gov.uk/vat/forms-rates/rates/rates-thresholds.htm

What VAT rates do I need to charge in the UK?

What you charge in VAT depends on what you are selling, and who you are selling to. If you are selling within the EU, then there are 3 rates of VAT. These rates are:

Standard Rate - 20%

At the present time the standard rate is 20% on most items. This is called the 'Standard rate' Prior to January 2011, the rate was 17.5%. Some economists have predicted a rate rise in the next couple of years, but there have been no plans announced by the government yet.

Reduced Rate - 5%

To qualify for reduced rate certain conditions have to be met. These conditions are affected by:

- who's providing them or buying them
- where they're provided
- how they're presented for sale
- the precise nature of the goods or services
- whether you obtain the necessary evidence
- whether you keep the right records

Examples of reduced rate goods are sales of new houses, energy saving materials such as loft insulation if they are installed in domestic houses (if they are installed in a prison they do not qualify), mobility aids for the elderly, electricity and gas for domestic customers and child car seats.

Zero Rate - 0%

There is a long list of items that qualify for zero rate tax, including financial services, cycle helmets, newspapers and magazines, children's clothing, parking spaces, aircraft repair and maintenance, domestic water supplies, low vision aids, advertising services for charities and most food and drink. Although alcohol has its own duty level and you have to pay standard rate tax on confectionery, sports drinks, ice cream, soft drinks and hot takeaways.

Tax Exempt and Outside the Scope of VAT

Some items are classed as tax exempt such as insurance or dental services. Other services are classed as 'outside the scope of VAT' - this includes charitable donations, road and bridge tolls, and selling personal possessions privately, or items sold outside of the EU.

There are some key differences between Tax exempt and Zero rated items. If you only sell tax exempt goods and services, then you cannot register for VAT. If you sell mainly zero rated items then you are taxed on a rate of zero, you can however apply to be exempt from registering for VAT in this case read this page for more information on the differences between zero-rated and tax exemption rules: https://www.gov.uk/vat-businesses

There is a full list of the VAT rates for goods on the HMRC website: https://www.gov.uk/rates-of-vat-on-different-goods-and-services

Do I Need to Show VAT Charges on my Ecom Website?

If you are VAT registered, then the prices displayed on the website must be VAT inclusive. If you sell to both trade and standard customers, then you can display an ex-vat price in addition, but the inc. VAT price must be clearly indicated.

International VAT Charges

If you are based in the UK and are selling goods within the EU, then you need to charge the domestic rate of VAT regardless of the member state's VAT rates. The amount you charge should be based on your home tax rules (see the tax rates section above).

Things start to get a bit more complicated when you have a business that has international connections. For example, if you have a server hosted in a different country, you cannot use the tax laws of that country to get away without paying VAT. It is where the business is based that determines the domesticity status. Even if you have registered a company in a different country, if your headquarters are based in the UK, or if you provide most of the services in the UK, then you are considered liable for UK tax.

US Nexus Regulations

If your e-commerce website sells to the United States, then normally you are considered to be an off-shore tax case. However there are cases where your business could be liable to pay local US tax. If you have any employees, business premises, or even if you heavily advertise in a particular state of the US, you can be asked to pay that state's tax rates. This is called the 'Nexus Law'.

The law was initially introduced in 1959 to cover goods and services that are offered in a particular state and to charge tax on those activities within their state. At the time, it was a relatively simple procedure to prove whether the business was liable under the Nexus Law, however, with the advent of online sales, this has become much more difficult to prove where the actual transaction takes place, for example if you are based in New York, and buy something from a UK based business as a present for your aunt living in California, where does the tax jurisdiction take place? From the vendor's perspective, the tax should be paid in the UK, but what if the supplier is also based in New York so when you buy the product, you are buying items in New York sending money to the UK, but the goods are shipped to California.

Most states are currently grappling with this problem and there is an excellent page here: http://www.cob.sjsu.edu/nellen_a/taxreform/economic_nexus.htm which shows what each state is doing to address the confusion.

Recently, Amazon was ordered by Pat Quinn, the governor of Illinois, to pay taxes on sales generated by affiliates based in the state because those affiliates constituted a business Nexus. Amazon responded by immediately sending a notification to terminate all affiliate accounts for the state.

It is entirely possible that if you start doing a lot of business with some US states then you may find yourself being considered under the Nexus law - especially if you generate more than £10,000 net income from those states. In this situation, you may find that you will have to alter your business to allow for such eventualities, possibly by splitting your business into different segments, or by targeting business to more tax friendly locations.

E-commerce Tax Off-Shore

Elsewhere in the world, there is some competition to entice international online companies to host their businesses in different countries and enjoy the lower tax, regulation relaxed, modern infrastructure environment. Gibraltar is one such country which has good links to the eurozone (although Spain has been a slight barrier to this free trade). If you are based in Gibraltar, then you pay less VAT, and lower international shipping charges.

EU Rules for Automated Digital Services

Recently, it was announced that all businesses registered in the UK which sell 'automated digital services' will have to register for tax, regardless of their income. Essentially the rules govern businesses that sell online content only, including apps, digital music files, e-books, website hosting, online courses, online advertising or any other product that is automatically generated. This means that many small businesses who fall beneath the £81,000 threshold will have to register for VAT. Additionally, if you sell to any country in the EU, then you have to charge the applicable tax in the recipient's county. With 28 member states in the EU, each with different vat rates and rules, this could become very tricky indeed. The Inland Revenue attempted to simplify this process by creating a Mini One Stop Shop (MOSS) which allows you to pay into a VAT account then the IR calculates the amount of tax applicable for each member state. https://www.gov.uk/register-and-use-the-vat-mini-one-stop-shop.

There is a campaign at the minute to change the rules for small businesses, as registering for VAT is an expensive and time consuming process. Dave Cameron has announced that he will raise the issue at the next summit in Brussels, but I wouldn't expect him to make much progress, especially many EU leaders look unfavourably on him after he used a veto block an EU treaty in 2011, and has committed himself to an EU membership referendum before the end of 2017.

In the meantime, if your business falls into this category, there are a few things you can do. Firstly, if you can, try to manually approve and deliver sales. For example, if you sell online courses, you could have a registration system that authorises funds, but requires you to manually capture the funds to approve the sale. One tactic is to write an email template, then when someone buys something from you, you physically send the email with the download link in it. Secondly, you could deliver a physical item to accompany your sale. Whether it's a printed certificate on completion of a course, a thank you letter or even a small postcard with their download password on it, it doesn't matter. If there is any manual activity that accompanies your business process, then you are excluded from the automated digital services rules.

Do I Need to Add VAT to Shipping Costs?

In the UK, the rules governing VAT charges on shipping are detailed on this page of the UK Customs website: https://www.gov.uk/government/publications/vat-notice-70024-postage-and-delivery-charges

At the minute, postal services offered by the Post Office are exempt from VAT (although this might change if the government decide to privatise this aspect of the Post Office). On 31st January 2011, the rules were changed so that special delivery and airsure are now standard rated.

If you are charging customers separately for postal services, then you might have to pay VAT depending on what you are sending. If you are delivering zero rated items like books then you do not pay VAT on the shipping costs. If you are sending standard rate items like jewellery, then you will have to pay VAT.

If you buy stamps from the post office as all or part of the shipping costs and then pass that cost on to your customers, then you need to add VAT on the whole price of the shipping.

What if I offer Free Delivery?

If your delivery cost is included with the price of items (e.g., if your ecommerce website includes a Free Delivery service) then the VAT is added to the whole of the price of the items and therefore, the tax implication is already catered for, so if you are selling books with free delivery, then no vat is added, but if you are selling DVDs including free delivery, then you need to add VAT to the total price.

What if there is a separate charge for packing or gift wrapping?

If you have a gift wrap option on your website, or if you have a separate charge for packing (eg if shipping delicate items you might add a surcharge to cover the extra padding costs), then the VAT rate is charged at the standard rate if the goods are to be delivered within the EU. This applies regardless of whether the items you are posting as standard rated or not. This is because you are offering a separately charged service and does not fall within a single contracted supply of goods.

What if I offer a 'pick up in-store' option

Essentially, you are making a single contracted supply of goods if your ecom website has to deliver the items to the recipients address (or their friends/relatives address or their own customers address) and if your website does not have a 'customer pickup' option. If you do offer a pickup service (e.g. if you run a small shop and offer the option of customers coming in to the shop to pick up their goods) then the option to deliver the items to the customer counts as an additional service and as such will be liable to VAT based on the nature of the delivered items. This is not affected by whether the charge you make for shipping is itemised separately or invoiced to the customer.

To be on the safe side, it is better to assume that you have to add VAT if the goods you are sending are rated for VAT.

What if I send both Zero rated and Standard rated items in the same shipment?

There is a lot of differing opinions online about how to handle mixed orders. According to some, if you ship differently rated items from your online store, the VAT on the shipping charge should be apportioned according to the items being delivered, so if you are posting on order including a £10 book and a £20 mug, then the book is zero rated and the mug is standard rated (20%). If your shipping cost is £6 then the VAT on postage should be calculated based on 2/3rds of the shipping cost - i.e. 20% of £4 = £0.80. Obviously you only have to add this VAT cost if you are VAT registered and posting items to destinations within the Eurozone. This sounds like the most sensible way to handle VAT on postage costs for Ecommerce websites.

Chapter 12. Customer Lifecycle Marketing

Ever read an article on marketing and not actually understood it? Even though you think you understand the meaning of the individual words, somehow then marketing folk string them together it makes no sense at all. This is because Marketing people use their own special kind of language. Like the way programmers use words like 'objects' and 'methods' to mean something completely different to what everyone else knows their meaning to be. Marketeers have their own special meanings for certain concepts. Often you will get a few acronyms thrown in too to confuse you further.

Customer lifecycle marketing articles are amongst the worst ones for this kind of behaviour. Instead of writing in plain English, these marketing experts seem to prefer to use jargon and short hand to convey their message in an esoteric way. So before explaining what customer lifecycle marketing (CLM) is, we should cover the common terms you might come across when researching it.

CRM – customer relationship management – this is the process by which a company manages it's interactions between current and future customers. Often this involves using technology to track when the customer has had any contact with the company, and who is responsible for looking after them.

CR- conversion rate (covered in the previous chapter) – basically the percentage of visits to your website that result in a sale.

RPV – Revenue per visit – how much each customer visit to your website is worth on average – this is a better measure of overall conversion rates as it takes into account the value of purchases, not only the number.

CLV – Customer Lifetime Value – basically a measure of how much that customer will be worth for the lifetime of their involvement with your company. If the customer makes a single one-off purchase, then the CLV is the same as the single sale. It is impossible to accurately predict future spending behaviour, but there is a method called predictive analytics then tries to do this.

Operating a business on a single sale process model is very inefficient. That's like throwing away your socks after wearing them every day and buying lots of new pairs. To increase your business value, you need to continue getting sales from the same customers as well as creating new customers. You cannot just rely on a single customer experience to get repeat custom. This is where CLM comes in.

12.1 Customer Evolution

In CLM, the customer passes through 5 distinct levels:

1. Prospect
2. Lead
3. Single purchase customer
4. Repeat customer
5. Loyal customer

In Customer Evolution, the customer is given a label which begins as a prospect and goes through each stage until they become a 'loyal customer'. The focus of your marketing is very much on advancing the person from one stage of the evolution to the next. Another phrase often used to describe this model is 'evolution marketing'.

At each stage of evolution you will lose customers. Not all prospects become leads, not all leads go on to purchase. So the focus of your efforts is to prevent as much leakage as possible from the stages. In this way, the CLV for each person is optimised.

12.2 The CLM marketing process

There are a number of different models for CLM marketing. One such model advocates a 5 stage process of:

1. Reach – getting the attention of people we want to reach
2. Acquisition – in an ecom website this means getting the people to visit the website
3. Conversion – getting the people to make a purchase
4. Retention – getting the people to buy more – e.g. cross selling, up-selling, discount codes etc.
5. Loyalty – getting the person to become more than a customer and because a 'brand ambassador' – e.g. advising friends to use your website or writing good reviews for your products.

A simpler model is that which proposes 3 stages:

1. Acquisition – getting leads
2. Activation – converting leads into customers
3. Retention and Loyalty – getting repeat customers

The two models are quite similar in their approach, although the first model is perhaps better in that it better fits the Evolution Marketing method.

For online businesses, there are 3 challenges:

1. How do we get people to visit the website?
2. How do we get people to buy things from the website?
3. How do we get people to come back and buy more?

Of the 3, the last one is the most significant. Getting people to come back and buy means you have won customer loyalty. This will increase the number of visits to the website from new customers if the loyal customer tells their friends. It also means that those visitors will have a higher opinion of the site and trust it more so will be more likely to purchase (challenge 2) and in turn they may because repeat customers if they have had a good buying experience. In this way, customer lifecycle can be seen as a circular process. At each stage of the process, your aim should be to prevent people from dropping off the cycle. This can be achieved by providing a good quality sale, and by following up on sales.

12.3 Post sale marketing

Many online businesses do not follow up on sales. They might add the customers email address to an email distribution list and send them the same batch email that they do to all their email subscribers. To increase return purchases, you need to focus more on what the customer is interested in. There are a few ways in which this can be done:

1. Interest based marketing – have different marketing lists for different interests, e.g. an email list for people who have previously bought bikes, and then another one for people who have previously bought car accessories – and then create different marketing emails for each.

2. Previous activity based marketing – Amazon is very good at this. If you look at watches on Amazon, then quite likely the next email you get will be 'hey look at these great watches'.

3. Staged marketing – this involves having a series of marketing messages (e.g. an email course) and after being added to the marketing list, the customer received these messages at regular intervals. This is quite effective in situations like pregnancy where you can send expectant couples a week by week update on what to expect from their stage of pregnancy.

4. Countdown marketing – can be used in cases such as when a subscription is about to end. An email is sent a few weeks before prompting them to update their subscription, then another a week before saying their subscription will end next week. Then a couple days before send a 'last chance to subscribe at the lower price' email, and then one after the subscription has ended to say 'Resubscribe now'

Whatever method you use, the important thing is that you continue your engagement with the customer. After working so hard to get the prospect to turn into a customer in the first place, it would be crazy not to keep them as a customer, because if you don't, someone else will.

Going Forward

Search Engine Optimisation and online marketing is a constantly shifting landscape. By the time you have read this book, it is possible that some of the information may be outdated. Google updates its ranking algorithm and services so frequently that anyone working in the industry has to spend a significant amount of time keeping up with the latest developments. In addition to this, internet trends and social media behaviour patterns change all the time. The best way to keep up is to subscribe to online marketing news feeds. Here's the sites that we check on a weekly basis:

1. Search Engine Land
   http://searchengineland.com

2. SEOmoz
   https://moz.com/blog

3. SEO Book
   http://www.seobook.com/blog

4. Search Engine Journal
   http://www.searchenginejournal.com/

5. Dave Naylor
   https://www.davidnaylor.co.uk/

6. Marketing Pilgrim
   http://www.marketingpilgrim.com/

Did you enjoy this book?

If you have found this book to be helpful, please let us know by posting a review on Amazon. Your feedback is important to us and will help us improve the quality of the publication. The volatile nature of online marketing means that the information in this book will need to be updated and amended on a regular basis. If you have purchased this book for your Kindle, you will be able to download the latest updates when they are released for free.

Updates to the paperback version will be made less frequently and if you want to be notified when the new edition of the book is available, please send an email to books@blackboxecom.com including your name, the version number of the book (shown on page 1) and your preferred email address. We will not share your details with anyone else and will not send you spam mails but may send you information and offers for other Blackbox publications and services, but only if you explicitly request this.

Hire Us

If you would like to hire Blackbox for SEO, online marketing, web design or bespoke online software, please visit www.blackboxecom.com and use the contact form on the website, or alternatively you can email us at info@blackboxecom.com

Thank you for reading this book, and please tell your friends and colleagues to buy a copy if you think they will find it useful.

www.ingramcontent.com/pod-product-compliance
Lightning Source LLC
LaVergne TN
LVHW022308060326
832902LV00020B/3337